DEBUNKING DETERMINISM

Robert Sapolsky, Sam Harris, and the
Crusade Against Free Will

DEBUNKING DETERMINISM

Robert Sapolsky, Sam Harris, and the
Crusade Against Free Will

David Lawrence

BP
Biochemical Press

Copyright © 2023 by David Lawrence
First edition: 2023

All rights reserved under International and Pan-American Copyright Conventions. No part of this book may be used or reproduced in any manner whatsoever, in any possible world or worlds, without written permission from the publisher, except in the case of brief quotations embodied in critical articles and reviews.

Library of Congress Cataloging-in-Publication Data
Name: Lawrence, David, author.
Title: Debunking Determinism: Robert Sapolsky, Sam Harris, and the Crusade Against Free Will
Description: New York: Biochemical Press
Identifiers: ISBN 979-8-9858769-5-6
Subjects: Philosophy | Psychology

Artwork by Dan Lovell

BIOCHEMICAL PRESS
New York, NY
10 9 8 7 6 5 4 3 2

TABLE OF CONTENTS

PREFACE XII

CHAPTER ONE WHAT'S IT ALL ABOUT? 23

Part One: Mother Theresa Meets Charlie Manson 23
    Enter Charlie Manson 2

Part Two: Who's Captaining the Ship? 3

Part Two: The Determinist View 4

Part Four: Squaring Off 6

Part Five: The Tentpole Arguments 8
    Morality and Personal Responsibility 10

CHAPTER TWO HARRIS V. SAPOLSKY 12

Part One: Harris Versus Sapolsky 13

Part Two: The Absolutist Conception of Choice 16
    The Significance of Limits and Constraints 22

Part Three: Sapolsky Science 22

Part Four: Biology and Environment 24
    Following Neural Commands 25
    Group Tendencies v. Individual Behavior 27
    Extraordinary Conditions, Extraordinary Results 30
    What's Happening on the Sidelines? 32

Part Five: The Bodily Platform 32

Part Six: It's Not About Math 34

Part Seven: The Missing Meaning 36
    Social Convention and Symbolic Significance 38

Part Eight: Conclusion 41

CHAPTER THREE THE MYTH OF CAUSATION 44

Part One: The World is a Machine 45

Part Two: Conceptual Problems 49
    From Plato to Newton 50

Part Three: Philosophical Problems 54
    Hume's Challenge 54
    Kant's Reply 55

Part Four: Causation and The Laws of Physics 57

Part Five: Lack of Scientific Relevance 59

Part Six: What's the Matter? 61

Part Seven: Conclusion 65

CHAPTER FOUR WHAT THE SCIENCE SAYS 67

Part One: Contemporary Scientific Fronts Against Causation 68
    Quantum Indeterminacy 68
    Relativity Theory 73

Part Two: Quantum Mechanics 73
    Twin Quantum Narratives 76
    Double Trouble 78
    Quantum Mysteries 81
    Schrödinger's Cat 83
    A Case Study – Many Worlds Interpretation 86

Part Three: Spooky Action 87
    Non-Local Influence 88
    Bell's Theorem and Spookiness 89

Part Four: For Whom Bell's Theorem Tolls 92

Part Five: Conclusion 94

CHAPTER FIVE THE SCIENCE OF FREE WILL............... 98

Part One: The Science Tests.. 99
The Headlines, Versus the Findings 102

Part Two: How the Studies Work... 104

Part Three: The Findings 105
The Libet Studies..105
The Haynes Study..110
The Fried Studies 112
Fried Hand Choice Study...114

Part Four: Causes, Correlations, and Prediction 115
Predictions..117
Discredited Methodology...118
Interpretation 120
Relevance..122
Selective Sequencing..123

Part Five: The Opposing Science 124
Random Fluctuations...124
Co-Variation...125
Post-RP Instructions...126
Decisions Not to Move..127
Reaction Studies 128

Part Six: Conclusion... 129

CHAPTER SIX.. 133

VIOLATING THE LAWS OF PHYSICS........................... 133

Part One: The Natural Order 134
What Did We Know 100 Years Ago? 137

Part Two: Cosmic Dominoes 140
    The Direction of Time 140
    No Single State of the Universe 142
    Random Events Versus Predetermination 144
    Micro Versus Macro Reality 145

Part Three: Strong Emergence 147

Part Four: Causal Circularity 153

Part Five: Undermining Science 154

Part Six: The Limits of Science 157
    How Does Water Freeze? 157

Part Seven: Conclusion 157

CHAPTER SEVEN 159

THE CONTRADICTORY NATURE OF DETERMINIST CLAIMS 159

Part One: The Fundamental Flaw 160

Part Two: Conventional Wisdoms 165

Part Three: Cultural and Political Contradictions 167

Part Four: Determinist Contradictions 168

Part Five: Don't Forget the Speaker 173

Part Six: Alien Control 176

Part Seven: Are We Really *Biochemical Robots*? 177
    The Perfect Prediction Machine 179
    Personal Identity 180
    I Think, Therefore Who Knows? 181

Part Eight: The Wasteland 182

Is the Use of Reason Reasonable? 183

Part Nine: Conclusion 184

CHAPTER EIGHT 187

HAVING IT BOTH WAYS 187

Part One: Try Acting Like a Determinist! 188

Part Two: *Free Will-Speak* 189

Part Three: Free Will-Speak Claims 190

Part Four: Is *Free Will-Speak* Shorthand? 206

Part Five: The Meditation Teacher 208

CHAPTER NINE 209

LOOK WHO'S TALKING! 209

Part One: Endorsing Free Will 210
    Determinist Persuasion 210

Part Two: Conclusion 213

CHAPTER TEN RESPONSIBILITY IN A CAUSAL UNIVERSE 215

Part One: The Irreconcilable Conflict 216
    Conceding the Problem 216
    Having Your Causal Cake 217
    Theories of Morality 221
    Utilitarianism and Determinism 223

Part Two: Pretending People Have Choice 226

How to See Others "As People" 228

Part Three: When Are We Responsible? 231

Part Four: When Are Others Responsible? 233
    Criteria for Responsibility 236

Part Five: Well-Being 236

Part Six: The Justice System 237
    Moral and Cultural Relativism 239

Part Seven: Conclusion 240

CHAPTER ELEVEN   KNOWING WHY 244

Part One: Why We Do Things? 245

Part Two: Decisions and Reasons 247
    Types of Explanations 248
    Types of Decisions 249
    The Problem With Practical Decisions 249
    Preference-Based Decisions 250
    Arbitrary Magic 252

Part Three: Essential Knowledge 255
    Our Next Thought 255
    Our Next Mental State 257
    Accounting for Success 258
    Knowing the Alternatives 259

Part Four: Conclusion 260

Predetermined Postscript 261

CHAPTER TWELVE OBSERVATION AND ENGAGEMENT 262

Part One: Watching Thoughts Arise 263

Authentic, or Illusory?.. 265

Part Two: The Neuroscience Findings 266

Part Three: Is *Free Will* a Feeling? 269

Part Four: Conclusion 271

CHAPTER THIRTEEN WHY DOES IT MATTER? 272

Part One: Determinism and Anti-Social Conduct 273
    The Science 273

Part Two: Losing the Belief in Free Will 275

Part Three: Conclusion 276

CHAPTER FOURTEEN 278

THE GREATEST STORY EVER TOLD 278
    State of Science 281
    Nature of Matter 283
    Nature of Consciousness 284

ENDNOTES 288

PREFACE

Why the need to debunk determinism?

First, because there's no compelling reason to believe it true and ample reason to believe it's not. Determinist doctrine leapfrogs over a host of unresolved scientific and philosophical questions. Determinist doctrine presumes to know what science concedes it doesn't.

Second, because it's a philosophy of disempowerment. Our lives are taken out of our hands. We think and do whatever causal forces dictate. We have no influence over others or worldly affairs. Everything is governed by a mechanical chain of physical events set in motion 13.8 billion years ago at the Big Bang.

In short, if determinism is true, we are utterly powerless. We blindly obey whatever physical forces demand.

This challenges the notion of personal responsibility. How can anyone be responsible for actions they didn't control and couldn't prevent? If our behavior is truly determined, we can't be any more responsible for our own actions than for anyone else's on the planet – we would equally lack control over both.

Morality fares no better. If determinism is true, our moral beliefs are dictated by causal events beyond our control. What we think about right and wrong is in the hands of predetermined physical forces – forces which have no conception of common decency, let alone moral conduct or the higher virtues. In a determined world, morality is based on causal compulsion, not moral truth.

And what are these forces of causal dominion?

They are blind, insentient, *physical events*. They don't think, feel, or reason. They have no regard for pain, misfortune, or destruction. They don't care about what's right or wrong and have no regard for consequences. They lack any sense of fair play or justice.

Under determinist doctrine, every aspect of our lives is controlled by such unthinking physical forces. They have no stake in human affairs. It doesn't matter to them if we're caused to lead fulfilling lives or to blow ourselves to smithereens.

Why should they care? How could they?

They aren't even *conscious*.

Sam Harris published *Free Will* in 2012.

Since then, he's become new media's most vigorous advocate against free will. Harris began his crusade by declaring the case against free will closed:

> *We know that determinism, in every way relevant to human behavior, is true. Unconscious neural events determine our thoughts and actions. (p. 16)* [1] *One fact now seems indisputable, some moments before you are aware of what you will do next...your brain has already determined what you will do. (p. 9)*

Free Will was a landmark event in popular discourse about the free will question. With but few exceptions, it was the first book aimed at a mainstream audience by a best-selling author. Moreover, it was articulate, accessible, and concise. For over a decade, it was one of a kind.

In fall of 2023, Harris' *Free Will* was joined by *Determined*, authored by neuro-endocrinologist and biologist Robert Sapolsky. *Determined* was the first popular polemic on behalf of determinist doctrine since the publication of *Free Will*.

With no less confidence than Harris, Sapolsky declares the free will question resolved:

> *All we are is the history of our biology, over which we have no control, and its interaction with the environment, over which we also have no control, creating who we are in the moment.*

By both accounts, the case is closed. Free will is a fantasy. Our fates were sealed for all eternity when the first glimmer of cosmic rays began emanating from the Big Bang. There's nothing to argue about.

Let's go home and see what's on Showtime.

If one were to accept the consequences, living in causal reality would be a nightmare. The fate of mankind would be in the hands of impersonal causal forces. Our sense of responsibility and moral beliefs would be dictated by insentient, physical events beyond our control.

Fortunately, we needn't worry. Determinism rest on unfounded assumptions about the nature of reality and human behavior. They don't hold up under scientific or philosophical scrutiny. At best, they are speculative resolutions to unresolved cosmic questions for which there is no answer.

The most fundamental of such presumptions concern the nature of *causation, matter, consciousness* in relation to the *current state of science,* in particular the laws of physics:

- ***Causation*** *is determinism's chief premise. Its meaning and existence are subject to philosophical and scientific dispute. The notion of causation is nowhere to be found in the fundamental laws of physics.*

- ***Matter*** *is what constitutes physical reality, that which causation would govern. It's nature is unknown – whether it consists of waves, particles, both, neither,*

- *strings, quantum fields, or something altogether different is an open scientific question.*

- **Consciousness** *is the ultimate cosmic mystery. How experience arises within a physical universe is unknown. The nexus of influence amongst consciousness and physical reality is an open scientific question.*

- **Physics** *doesn't know whether the universe is deterministic or probabilistic. The fundamental laws of physics don't require that time run forward or that causes need precede effects.*

These statements are not matters of dispute. They reflect the state of science and current limits of human knowledge. Each alone undermines the credibility of determinist doctrine.

In a nutshell:

- *If we don't know what causation means or whether it exists, how can we know whether it governs the universe?*

- *If we don't know what matter is, how can we know whether it's capable of being governed by causation?*

- *If we don't know the nature of consciousness, how can we know whether free will is, or isn't, one of its most fundamental attributes?*

- *If we don't know whether reality is deterministic, how can we know whether the world is predestined and human behavior the result of prior causal conditions?*

Rather than offering support, the present state of science undermines the credibility of determinist claims. In a nutshell, bold declarations that the world is mechanical and human behavior determined lack scientific validation.

Putting it all together, the big picture challenge to determinist doctrine can be summarized as follows:

If the concept of causation is problematic, if the nature of matter is unknown, if consciousness and the existence of subjective experience is inexplicable, if science doesn't know whether the universe is deterministic, and if the fundamental laws of physics don't require "causes" to precede "effects" – how can anyone credibly claim to know that reality unfolds in successive predetermined states and that human behavior is determined?

Determinism is challenged by a greater problem. In this case, it isn't capable of being resolved by obtaining further knowledge:

Determinist claims are *self-contradictory*.

If our thoughts and actions are byproducts of physical force, this would include our beliefs *about what's true*. We believe true whatever predetermined physical events dictate. In a predetermined universe, there's no basis by which anyone could believe anything true *other than causal force*.

Hence the self-contradiction present in all truth claims made by determinist advocates:

> **Determinism is true. How do I know it? I'm causally compelled to believe it true by physical events over which I have no control. But you can believe me, it really is true. . . .**

Determinism thus disqualifies its own adherents from claiming it true. By their own terms, determinists are *forced to believe* in determinism. They were *predetermined* to believe free will is nonsensical. Had they been predestined to believe in the human capacity for choice, they'd just as boldly declare it to be true.

In short, by removing any rational basis for believing anything true, determinism invalidates all truth claims – *including its own*.

The contradiction is thus inescapable: if determinism were true, the belief in determinism *would be a causal byproduct over which determinists could have no control*. Tomorrow they might be caused to believe in free will. Or perhaps in 10 minutes.

Why not? If you're a determinist, there's no reason to believe you'll remain so for any length of time. There's no telling what you might believe in 10 minutes. It depends on, and *only* on, what you were predestined to believe....

Popular determinist advocacy isn't troubled by such concerns. Most of them aren't on the radar. Determinist premises are largely treated as givens, and rarely given serious critical scrutiny. Popular discourse gives them a free pass.

Thus unaccountable, determinists ignore the larger scientific context. Declarations about the genesis of human behavior sit atop more foundational cosmic questions which remain unresolved, including the origin of the universe; the nature of physical reality; the genesis of life from matter; the genesis of consciousness from life; and the adaptive value, if any, provided by subjective experience. That the free will question is dependent on the answer to more fundamental cosmic questions goes without comment in popular discourse.

In the midst of grappling with foundational cosmic conundrums, the scientific home front is beset with its own set of problems:

- *The two most successful scientific theories of all time – relativity and quantum mechanics – are at loggerheads about the nature of reality. Science offers not one, but two conflicting laws of physics.*

- *The "Standard Model" of elementary particles, which catalogues the fundamental constituents of the universe,*

> *contains over a dozen parameters which can't be explained, including relations among the four fundamental forces of nature.*

- *Quantum science is itself stuck between two conflicting narratives. Reality evolves in wave-like fashion, but upon measurement only particles appear. Over two dozen conflicting quantum theories are competing for official recognition. Some are deterministic, others probabilistic.*

Hence the big picture doesn't bode well for determinist premises. They skip past more than a handful of foundational cosmic mysteries on whose resolution the free will question *depends*. A sober assessment of human knowledge demands a humbler attitude. More homework needs to be done.

Unless you're prepared to take shortcuts, a credible answer to the free will question awaits another day.

Since publishing *Free Will,* Sam Harris has been spreading determinist gospel far and wide. Dozens of *YouTube* videos offer lectures, debates, interviews, and podcasts in which he confidently declares free will illusory. Robert Sapolsky has joined the party and is presently spreading the gospel of causation with no less abandon and enthusiasm.

The reception that greeted *Free Will*, and now underway for *Determined*, has been virtually devoid of critical challenge. [2] Sapolsky has been welcomed as the new celebrated Emeritus of club-determinism. Podcast hosts like Laurence Krauss enthusiastically join him in sounding the death knell for human choice. Not a single serious doubt or concern is expressed during their dialogue about the integrity of determinist premises.

Hence the purpose of this discussion: to examine the critical flaws in determinist thinking, flaws remaining conspicuously absent from popular dialogue.

The lack of serious challenge to *Free Will* and *Determined* is hard to explain. Determinist premises are scientifically uncertain. Determinist arguments are largely circular. Determinist evidence is generated by self-fulfilling, selective interpretations. Scientific references are often inaccurate or incomplete.

The following discussion is preoccupied by these and similar claims. They are matters of no small concern to the free will debate.

Free Will and *Determined* ignore the bulk of them. They nevertheless remain standing in the wings of popular discourse, yet to be afforded the opportunity of making an entrance.

Harris and Sapolsky confidently endorse determinist doctrine. Human behavior is determined, and that's that.

This discussion reflects a different kind of advocacy. It argues against the merits of determinism while mindful that free will has its own set of problems. It's not the ideal candidate, nor any less immune to critical scrutiny. Like most elections, taking sides in the free debate is about voting against those least qualified for office, not endorsing the perfect candidate.

Two types of arguments are generally interwoven in considering the subject of free will: (1) those that give cause to doubt determinist doctrine, and (2) those that give reason to believe in free will. The two are related, but the former doesn't always imply the latter – arguments against determinism don't demonstrate, let alone provide any degree of certainty, that humans have the capacity for choice.

The counter-arguments in this discussion thus aren't presented or presumed to be definitive. They are first and foremost offered to demonstrate that (1) determinist claims presume to know the answer to fundamental cosmic questions that remain unresolved; that (2) the issues involved in the free will debate are far more complex and nuanced than how they're portrayed in popular determinist advocacy; and that (3), as a consequence of the foregoing, determinists must necessarily cut corners in making their case – avoiding essential questions, failing to troubleshoot premises, neglecting to address many of the most serious opposing considerations, and ignoring critical context.

What's missing is a healthy dose of agnosticism – not only due to the state of science, but by virtue of the answer remaining elusive after more than two millennia of debate. This may suggest the need for a new conceptual paradigm, unconstrained by current preconceptions about the nature of reality. Solving the free will problem may require new connections among events which transcend the confines of random, probabilistic, causal, chaotic, and volitional relations.

They don't seem to be doing the trick.

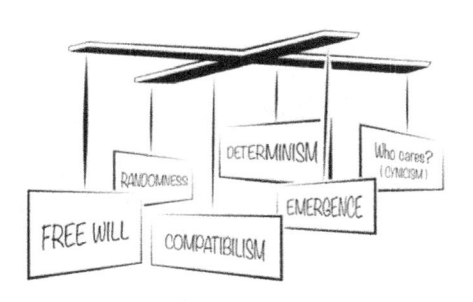

Chapter One
WHAT'S IT ALL ABOUT?

Part One: Mother Theresa Meets Charlie Manson

Mother Teresa was born in Kosovo at the turn of the last century. She achieved worldwide fame for helping the poor and destitute. Her humanitarian efforts spanned the globe and she was canonized a saint in 2016.

The good Mother is praised for her tenacious devotion to helping the less fortunate. But what if she had no choice? What if she had no control over her actions?

Imagine she had a chip implant. Suppose a team of scientists had always controlled her thoughts and actions. Everything she ever did was forced upon her without her consent. Would we still think she deserved our praise if we learned she never once chose to help anyone – that she was coerced into being charitable and compassionate?

Would her saintly deeds still seem so saintly?

Enter Charlie Manson

Now imagine Charlie Manson had a similar implant. Suppose he had been forced to do everything he ever did. Suppose he never chose to hurt anyone, let alone murder them.

Would there be any difference between him and Mother Theresa? What could it be?

Both their thoughts and actions would be in the hands of unknown outside forces. Neither would have any say in their behavior. Neither could do otherwise than as instructed by their scientific puppeteers.

Indeed, the chip implant would dissolve all distinctions between them. The only difference would be what they were forced to do, over which neither one of them had the least bit of control.

Manson was given a set of malevolent instructions – but that wasn't his fault. Mother Theresa was given the benevolent ones – but, as with Manson, she had nothing to do with her instructions.

They both did what they did because they were forced to and couldn't have done otherwise.

Neither *had any choice*.

Now, substitute *physical causes* for the chip implant.

Imagine that such causes are part of a long physical chain of causation extending back to the Big Bang.

As with the chip implant, nobody would control anything they think or do. Nobody would be responsible for their actions, which would be dictated by outside forces. Nobody would be any more virtuous or malevolent than anyone else, no matter what they did – our actions wouldn't express who we are, but who we were *predestined to be.*

Whether by chip or causal force, the result is the same – we're under the causal dominion of cosmic forces we don't control.

Our lives aren't our own.

This is the gospel of determinism. I don't control what I'm writing right now, and you don't control whatever you're thinking about what you're reading.

So, while you may not have any choice about it:

Welcome to the free will debate.

Part Two: Who's Captaining the Ship?

Where do our thoughts and actions come from?

Suppose you're drinking lemonade. You decide to take another sip and reach for the glass. What made that happen?

For the free will advocate, you decided to quench your thirst and deliberately grabbed the glass. The source of your action was conscious choice, the exercise of free will.

If you're a determinist, physical forces caused your thirst and the desire to quench it. The movements made by your arm were dictated by prior conditions, by neural activity and other physical forces.

This is what the free will debate is about. Do we have a hand in how we behave, or are we biochemical puppets, forced to comply with whatever blind physical forces demand?

This depends in large measure on who or what's steering the cosmic ship. With respect to human behavior, the top contenders for the captainship include:

- **Causal Force**
- **Free Will**
- **Randomness**
- **Biology and Environment**
- **Subatomic Reality**
- **Birth circumstances and personal history**
- **Some combination of the above**
- **Divine Will**
- **Something Unknown or Unknowable**

Part Two: The Determinist View

Aside from free (and divine) will, the list consists of *physical phenomena* comprised of physical forces and. Along with a smattering of randomness, determinists believe that everything has a *physical cause*.[1]

With respect to human behavior, several causal sources are including among the forefront. Harris and Sapolsky alternate amongst them as suits the occasion. While there's both overlap and tension amongst them, they can be loosely sorted as follows:

- ***Biology and environment***: genome, neurophysiology, evolutionary heritage, physical conditions, culture, etc.

- ***Personal Factors***: Birth circumstances, parents, childhood upbringing, economic class, etc.

- ***Subatomic Activity***: The subatomic play of elementary particles, which generate all macro-level events, including our thoughts and behavior.

- ***The Cosmic Causal Chain***: Each state of the universe causes each subsequent state, in a succession of moments from the Big Bang to the present. Full knowledge of any given state would permit the prediction of all future states.

A truly impressive list. Their collective powers appear formidable and inescapable. Whether that's the case is the subject of this discussion.

Part Four: Squaring Off

There are three main combatants in the battle over the human capacity to exercise free will.

They are usually defined as follows:

Determinism

Everything that happens is attributable to prior conditions operating under the laws of physics. Biological and environmental sources are amongst such conditions. Our thoughts and actions were predestined some 13.8 billion years ago. But for a smattering of randomness, nothing can be diverted off the predetermined path. We have no influence over our destinies.

Free Will (Libertarian)

The commonsense notion. We have the ability to form intentions, make choices, initiate actions, and influence the course of worldly affairs. Within limits and constraints, we can *choose otherwise*. Choice is part of the natural order, even if science doesn't yet understand how it all works.

While there are other definitions, *libertarian free will* offers true "liberty", i.e., the ability to do otherwise without being entirely bound by prior conditions and present circumstances.

Compatibilism

The conflict between choice and causation is misguided. Free will is simply the ability to act in satisfaction of our desires, under conditions without internal or external constraints (e.g., mental disorder, handcuffs, etc.) If I want more lemonade and nothing prevents my reaching for the glass, I'm exercising free will – even if my desires and actions are determined by causal events beyond my control and notwithstanding that I lack the ability to do otherwise.

Two's Company, Three's Incompatible

Harris and Sapolsky both reject *compatibilism*.

They agree that the attempt to reconcile choice and causation is a cheap parlor trick that misdirects the mind: either we have the ability to choose otherwise in the face of prior conditions or we don't.

We can't both live in a mechanical universe where we don't control our thoughts or actions, *and have* the capacity for choice. Indeed, being controlled by unthinking physical events is precisely what free will *isn't*.

Compatibilism attempts to reconcile causal hegemony and free will by redefining what it means to exercise choice. Free will is construed as the unfettered ability, at a given moment, to satisfy one's desires – regardless of their source. Harris calls the definition a "bait and switch". He rightfully notes that this isn't what anyone means by the capacity to freely choose. Sapolsky agrees, catchily remarking that "compatibilism is *incompatible* with the way the world works".

Polls seem to suggest compatibilism is the predominate view among scientists and philosophers. Fortunately, such matters aren't resolved by election. This author agrees with Harris and Sapolsky that compatibilism is a sleight-of-hand which ducks the question and isn't the solution. Since there's no need to critique their position on the matter, the discussion which follows doesn't concern itself with compatibilist doctrine.

Part Five: The Tentpole Arguments

Harris and Sapolsky marshal a handful of overlapping arguments in support of determinist doctrine.

The most prominent can be summarized as follows:

Argument #1: Complete Control

Free will requires complete control over everything that would otherwise determine our thoughts and actions, which we clearly don't have.

Argument #2: Biology and Environment

Free will is precluded because our thoughts and actions are generated by biology mixed with environment – e.g., genes, neurophysiology, hormonal function, etc. interacting with environmental conditions.

Argument #3: Determinism is True, No Room Left For Free Will

The universe unfolds in a global chain of physical events dating back to the Big Bang. Everything that happens is dictated by prior physical conditions operating under the laws of physics. There's *no room left* for the operation of free will.

Argument #4: The Neuroscience Studies

Neuroscience studies of neural brain activity demonstrate that prior increases in neural activity cause our decisions before we're aware of what our decisions and subsequent actions will be.

Argument #5: Watching Thoughts Arise

Inner experience demonstrates that we don't originate or control our thoughts, we passively *watch them arise* before us from sources outside consciousness.

Argument #6: Violating the Laws of Physics

The universe is driven by physical activity operating under the laws of physics. Conscious intervention in the physical world would disrupt those laws, by which only physical events have influence.

Argument #7: Not Knowing Why

Free will would require *knowing why* we do things and, accordingly, the ability to explain our actions. We are unable to do so – we can only relate after-the-fact "stories" about why we did what we did.

Morality and Personal Responsibility

No discussion of free will is complete without addressing the issue of morality and personal responsibility. They are thorns in the side of determinism.

How can we be responsible for our actions or abide by moral principles if we have no control over our thoughts, intentions, or actions?

Determinists are tasked with explaining how such notions make sense in a world where our thoughts and actions are dictated by external forces. How can the existence of morality and moral truth be justified in a world where *all our beliefs* – including what's right, wrong, just, and immoral – are caused by physical events beyond our control and we lack any ability to think otherwise?

Even if we were to stumble upon a credible source of moral guidance, determinists are called upon to explain how such a source could be of any help if nobody controls their intentions or actions, and thus without any ability to follow such guidance.

———

That concludes the intro –

The problem, possible solutions, main schools of thought, issues of morality and responsibility, and tentpole determinist arguments against free will.

Stage now set, it's time to proceed to the matters at hand.

Granted, it may be we have no choice….

Chapter Two
HARRIS V. SAPOLSKY

THE HEADLINES

Sapolsky and Harris take different paths, but share a half dozen fundamental misconceptions about how to construe the facts. Sources of influence are mistaken for forces of control. Correlations are confused with causation. Probabilistic trends are offered as evidence that all individual behavior in concrete circumstances is causally compelled. Universal behavioral processes are inferred from multi-trial averages of diverse individual responses. Limits and constraints are misconstrued as preventing choice, rather than facilitating it. Evidence is generated by interpreting facts through determinist premises. In the midst of all this, credible evidence that causal forces determine all human behavior is nowhere to be found.

Part One: Harris Versus Sapolsky

Not all determinists are created alike.

Harris and Sapolsky reject both libertarian and compatibilist versions of free will. But they often part ways when it comes to emphasis, arguments, and degree of certainty about our lack of free will.

Amongst the two, Harris is the true believer. He considers our lack of capacity for choice "indisputable": we don't control our thoughts, don't control our actions, and have no influence over worldly affairs. That's the way it is, deal with it.

We know that determinism...is true. It's "indisputable" that our brains make our decisions. (p. 13)

The future is set – and this includes all our future states of mind and our subsequent behavior. (p. 29)

Sapolsky is more cautious, less confident. He acknowledges there are troubling uncertainties about the issue and pending questions whose answers are less than entirely satisfactory. In short, there's still "wiggle room". In the end, he rises above his doubts and casts his vote along party lines with Harris:

If you focus on any single field...you are left with plenty of wiggle room for deciding that biology and

> *free will can coexist. But...put all the scientific results together... and there's no room for free will. These disciplines collectively negate free will because they are all interlinked... (p. 8)*

While the arguments overlap, each has his own particular take. Sapolsky leans heavily on science. He offers a host of data about biochemical, neurological, and environmental influences. For him, biology is destiny – with a healthy dose of environmental influence:

> *Biology over which you had no control, interacting with environment over which you had no control, made you you. (p. 3)*

Harris' approach is more eclectic. In addition to science, he looks to philosophy, inner experience, and the inability to explain our actions. He proposes stringent criteria for free will's existence, setting a bar too high to be met. He looks to inner experience, claiming we passively observe our *thoughts arising* without any sense of authorship. He argues against free will on the basis that we can't explain our actions – we can only give after-the-fact "stories" about why we did what we did.

Both call upon a long line of neuroscience findings dating back to the mid-1980's. As discussed in Chapter Five, their presentations are selective and inaccurate. The findings they cite refuse to endorse determinism, fail to find causal connections between neural activity and decisions, rely on a discredited central measurement, and provide substantial evidence against neural brain determinism. Sapolsky concedes the studies are problematic and discusses some of their key flaws and various objections within the neuroscience community. Harris ignores them, failing to inform his readers of the many credible contrary studies which offer serious challenges to the few that he cites.

———

Harris and Sapolsky part ways most when it comes to the matter of personal responsibility and morality. While they end up offering similar suggestions, their positions are fundamentally opposed to each other.

Harris confidently maintains that morality and personal responsibility survive a predetermined universe:

> *If we remain committed to seeing people as people, we can find some notion of personal responsibility that fits the facts. (p. 49)*

Sapolsky just as adamantly insists that morality and responsibility can't be reconciled with causal reality:

> *There's no free will, and thus holding people morally responsible for their actions is wrong. [That's] where I sit. (p. 11)*

Notwithstanding opposing viewpoints, both set forth a robust patchwork of recommendations that include deterring harm, protecting the innocent, addressing the causes of crime, rejecting the role of retribution, etc. Harris proposes we *pretend* people have free will and use the "conventional outline" to assess responsibility. Sapolsky suggests we take action to "quarantine" those who would likely harm others again.

These and similar suggestions boldly violate determinist doctrine – how can we protect others from harm or seek to implement such social policies if we don't control our thoughts or actions, not to mention that all human behavior was "set" at the Big Bang?

These problems are addressed in Chapter Seven, *Moral Responsibility in a Mechanical Universe*.

Part Two: The Absolutist Conception of Choice

Harris and Sapolsky conceive of free will in absolutist terms. It's an *all or nothing* proposition.

Harris asks "what it would take" to have free will. He maintains it would require *complete control* over what determines our thoughts and actions.

You would need to be aware of all the factors that determine your thoughts and actions, and you would need to have complete control over those factors. (p. 13)

That's one tall order. It's far afield of commonsense, and more than a little counter-intuitive. Control *everything*, or control *nothing*. The claim is overtly circular – it presumes from the get-go that we're controlled by outside "factors" and lack the ability to influence reality:

What would it take to have free will? That we not be determined by the factors that control us.

Harris sums up his *all or nothing* conception of free will on a Lex Fridman's podcast:

You can get at this conceptually and unravel the notion of free will.... I didn't make myself, I didn't make my genes, I didn't make my brain, I didn't make the environmental influences...and yet these are the only things that can contrive to produce my next thought or impulse or behavior.[1]

As a factual matter, naturally Harris is correct. We didn't "make" our genes, brains, or environment. What *doesn't* follow is that *they alone* "contrive to produce" our behavior. This is a determinist conclusion, not an argument for the causal cause. Harris peppers *Free Will* with similar claims, which sound like arguments but which presume determinist premises true:

> *If a man's choice to shoot the president is determined by a certain pattern of neural activity", how can we say, "that his will is 'free'? (p. 5)*

The answer is obvious. We can't.

But this isn't evidence against free will. The question assumes we don't have it – that the man's choice *was determined* by neural activity. Harris isn't offering an argument, but a conclusion based on determinist premises:

> **If the man's choice to shoot someone was determined by neural brain activity and not the exercise of free will, then how can you say he has free will?**

If such claims were backed by supportive arguments, they would qualify as conclusions. As we shall see, they are surrounded by similar conclusory declarations which sound like arguments but which reflect determinist presumptions.

Sapolsky likewise embraces an absolutist conception of free will. The capacity for choice would require we be entirely unaffected by prior constraints and influences:

In order to prove there is free will, you have to show that some behavior just happened out of the thin air... Free will can exist only neurons actions are completely uninfluenced by all the uncontrollable factors that came before... (p. 83)

Harris' and Sapolsky's absolutist conception of free will disregards the distinction between *influence* with *control*. Factors of influence, which constrain and circumscribe behavior, are construed as forces of control which determine what we do.

The presumption that influence means control results in factual interpretations which ratify determinist premises because they stem from them. It can't be otherwise: separating influence from control would allow for the possibility of choice in areas beyond the bounds of identified influences. Construing influence as control precludes the ability to resist the forces of our biological and environmental heritage. Sapolsky thus insists we lack the "grit" to do so:

Fighting biology: *Do you have grit?* Destructive sexual urges: *Do you resist acting upon them?* Marathon running: *Do you fight through pain?* Not being bright: *Do you triumph by studying extra hard?* Fighting alcoholism: *Do you order ginger ale instead?* [No], you can't. (p. 93, quotes are in italics)

We're thus left with the "emerging mantra" he repeats throughout *Determined*:

All we are as the history of our biology, over which we had no control, and of its interaction with environments, over which we also had no control, creating who we are in the moment. (p. 85)

There are no influences of *mere* influence. There are only factors of determination. Harris and Sapolsky thus devote themselves to cataloguing the many aspects of our lives over which we clearly have little or no control. But parading a long list of constraints on behavior doesn't demonstrate behavior's determined. It demonstrates that we're susceptible to many influences, both profound and trivial.

Held to scrutiny, the *all or nothing* conception of choice leads to absurd results. The single most determinant factor in our lives is the Big Bang. It scattered the cosmic seeds in a way that permitted the development of life and, ultimately, our own life form. In order to control all determinant factors, we'd have to control the Big Bang. Having free will would require giving birth to the cosmos. We would need to be omniscient and omnipotent.

In short, we'd have to be God.

This seems overly ambitious. Do we really have to create the cosmos to scramble up some eggs for breakfast?

Free will advocates don't deny that our lives are affected by numerous factors beyond our control. It's true, we can't flap our arms and fly. It's true, we aren't likely to become an NBA superstar if we're born 5 feet 2. It's true, we can't change the force of gravity and jump to the moon. But such constraints don't evidence the lack of free will absent circular determinist interpretation. They evidence the obvious – that there are practical limits to the capacity for choice, natural constraints imposed by conditions, boundaries, capabilities, heritage, and circumstances.

In the free will paradigm, our bodies a platform on which conscious activity operates. Biology and environment are construed as dressing the stage on which the game of life is played. Nothing about this narrative is any less consistent with the facts than foregone determinist interpretations.

Don't think I'm against omniscience.

It would save me from having to search for my iPhone five times a day.

The Significance of Limits and Constraints

The B side to the *all or nothing* conception of free will is equally unsound: the presumption that free will can't operate if subject to conditions, limitations, or constraints.

This gets it backwards:

Free will *couldn't operate* without such limitations.

Choice requires that reality be structured. It can't operate in a vacuum. Limits and constraints are what brings structure to reality. The resistance of the track allows the runner to spring forward. The resistance of the clay permits the sculptor to fashion it into the desired shape. The resistance of the violin strings allows the musician to create vibrations that deliver sound waves to the ear.

It's the *lack of complete control* which structures reality and provides circumstances. Without limiting conditions and circumstances, there would be no prerogatives.

Influences are constraints, which *make free will possible*.

Part Three: Sapolsky Science

Sapolsky's scientific approach does nothing to dispel these conceptual presumptions. It's based on them, and then some.

The evidence he offers consists of factual interpretations run through the determinist mill. The *not-so-short* list of causal confusions behind Sapolsky-science:

- *Adding up behavioral influences doesn't amount to determined behavior.*

- *Tendencies, trends, and group behavioral patterns don't evidence causation and don't translate into individual behavior.*

- *The ability to predict behavior isn't evidence that it's determined.*

- *Evidence that some behavior is causally determined is not evidence that all behavior is causally determined.*

- *Behavior under extraordinary conditions is not representative of behavior under ordinary or optimal conditions.*

- *Behavior induced by mental or physical dysfunction is not representative of non-impaired or functional behavior.*

- *The immediate impact that neural, hormonal, and other biochemical activity can have on consciousness is not evidence that such activities cause behavior.*

- *Evidence based on circular reasoning isn't evidence. It's as the name suggests.*

These and similar misconceptions serve to frame the facts in a manner which supports determinist premises.

As a consequence, the bulk of science data offered by Harris and Sapolsky is beside the point and none of it demonstrates that human behavior is determined.

Part Four: Biology and Environment

Determined takes us on a spirited romp through the brain, neural system, hormones, and more.

A lot of facts are thrown at us. Many of them are interesting. Many of them are fascinating. None of them demonstrate our behavior is determined.

Did you know judges tend to give harsher sentences when they've skipped lunch, or when a bad smell's in the courthouse? Next time you're called to court, don't forget to shower, and bring an apple or two for the judge.

Is it any surprise that hunger or bad smells make us irritable? Or that when we're jangled or uncomfortable, our better angels are replaced by even better devils?

This and similar examples contain no evidence that behavior is determined. It's evidence that we get cranky when we don't attend to biological needs and are susceptible to environmental irritants. It doesn't preclude our choosing how and when we deal with them – let alone preclude the possibility that our *prior choices* factor into getting us to where we are in the first place.

Yet these and a boatload of similar examples are touted as evidence that all human behavior is determined.

If you're not irritated by that, then you probably had a big lunch and are reading this while outdoors enjoying the fresh air.

Following Neural Commands

Sapolsky provides a bounty of information that link neural brain activity to thoughts and behavior.

The prefrontal cortex (PFC) takes center stage in Sapolsky's discussion. The amygdala plays Robin to PFC's Batman.

The PFC is involved in executive function, decision-making, learning, inhibiting wrong behavior, reigning in emotions, fighting temptation, learning new rules, social functioning. The amygdala is associated with emotional processing, including fear and anxiety.

Sapolsky relates their functions in anthropomorphic terms, indicating they're calling the shots.

Some of many examples:

- The PFC shuts down amygdala activity when we're thinking bad thoughts, telling us: "Don't think that way. That's not who I am". (p 96)

- When the amygdala fires up fearing social ostracism, the PFC steps in to clamp it down, telling us: "Get this in perspective; this is just a stupid game". (p. 96)

- A subregion of the PFC, the vmPFC, supplies our "gut feelings" when questions of strategy are at issue: "How will I feel if I do X and Z then happens?" (p. 101)

Naturally the dialogue is metaphorical, but it assumes true what Sapolsky's attempting to prove – that there's a *causal relationship* between neural brain activity and everything we think and do. But the fanciful dialogue reflects a causal *interpretation* of such neural brain activity, not evidence that demonstrates any such causal connection.

Sapolsky views the PFC as *commanding* us to "get things in perspective", etc. He dismisses any role for deliberation, weighing of consequences, application of values, and choice. Nothing *in facts* demonstrates that these factors are absent. Nothing *in the facts* provides *any basis on which to eliminate* the possibility that the change in perspective resulted from a volitional process culminating in an all-things-considered choice based on circumstances.

The facts are susceptible to both interpretations – outcome by neural command, or outcome by deliberative processes underpinned by neural activity. Sapolsky's conclusion isn't derived from factual evidence and isn't the result of factual inference. It a determinist interpretation which superimposing a determinist overlay from the determinist playbook.

Determined is filled with such circular descriptions, which inevitably lead to conclusions which presumes determinism true and don't demonstrate what they're offered to prove. None of them eliminate contributions from volitional activity.

At least that's what my amygdala is telling me....

Group Tendencies v. Individual Behavior

Most of the data presented by Sapolsky concerns *possible* or *probable* outcomes. The findings catalogue trends, tendencies, and likelihoods. They are statistical patterns concerning probabilistic group or individual behavior.

They aren't about causal relations and do nothing to demonstrate that behavior is determined.

Some of many examples:

- When faces of other races are flashed, the amygdala activates *in 70%* of subjects.

- Subjects cued by the world "ocean" are *more likely* to identify "Tide" as their detergent of choice.

- A *substantial percentage* of criminals committing violent crimes have a history of brain trauma. (p. 99)

- Adolescent experiences [play] an *outsized role* in constructing the frontal cortex.

- Religious people *tilt in the direction of* valuing obedience, loyalty, and purity. (p. 258)

- As for judges, well, you've already been warned about that one....

What does any of this have to do with free will? What in any of this data demonstrates that human behavior is determined?

Nothing. No such findings translate into how *any given individual* will *actually behave* in *specific situations.*

Being in the 70% group of "face flash" responses says nothing about how anyone in the group goes about their life – let alone behave under circumstances in which such factors might come into play.

In the free will paradigm, such probable outcomes in large measure reflect choices, actions, and values, along with a fair share of indoctrination and influence. Nothing precludes contributions from intentions and choice from factoring into any of these statistics.

Having assumed from the get-go that neural activity causes our experiences free of any influence from non-physical meanings or volitional activity, Sapolsky issues the following challenge to free will advocates:

Find me the neuron that started [an action] ...show me [it was not] influenced by whether the man was tired, hungry, stressed...[that] this neuron's function was [not] altered by...sights, sounds, smells ...hormones...genes...experiences during his childhood...centuries of history and ecology... culture in which he was raised....and then we can talk about free will....

Free will requires the spontaneous burst of *ex nihilo* neural activity. Putting aside the circular presumptions, the scientific evidence isn't there. Free will advocates can readily respond to Sapolsky's *find me the neuron* challenge as follows:

Find me the scientific data identifying the neuron or neurons responsible for causing specific individuals, in specific circumstances, to behave in specific ways, culled from a sampling sufficient to evidence the causal genesis of behavior across all individuals, all conditions and contexts, and for all behavioral types - and we can talk about the idea that all human behavior is determined. . . .

None of the evidence set forth in *Determined* is up to the challenge. Probabilistic behavior based on group averages culled from diverse individual responses, along with anthropomorphic interpretations of neural activity that preclude volitional contributions in order to prove the lack of volitional contribution, aren't up to the task.

Sapolsky's and Harris' examples leave more than ample room for free will.

Extraordinary Conditions, Extraordinary Results

Free Will and *Determinism* call upon aberrant behavior under abnormal conditions to demonstrate our behavior is determined. Such behavior says nothing about the genesis of functional behavior under normal conditions.

Harris begins his book recounting the true story of two psychopaths who engaged in a horrific killing spree that resulted in the brutal deaths of a family on a tragic evening. He attributes their behavior to a combination of genes, life experience, and brain state. (p. 4) Later, he poses a hypothetical about a man with a "golf ball" size tumor who kills a young woman "for the fun of it". We're told her death would be "the result of events arising in the brain". (p. 50 – 51)

Choosing your toothpaste is thus no different than killing someone under the influence of a tumor. It's just another action resulting from neural brain events.

Similarly, Sapolsky turns to dysfunctional cases (not involving toothpaste) and painstakingly recounts the medical history involved in treating epilepsy and schizophrenia. Back in the day, epilepsy was attributed to "demons". In the not-so-distant past, schizophrenia was attributed to "terrible mothering". Fathers got off the hook because they were "passive and henpecked".

Needless to say, medicine has long since left the land of demons and hen-pecking. Now, epilepsy and schizophrenia are generally attributed to "an unlucky combination of genes... neurotransmission and brain development". (Sapolsky, p. 332). Mothers, you're finally off the hook.

The medical history may be fascinating but says *nothing* about free will. It illustrates the obvious – that overwhelming influence can diminish or preclude the ability to act rationally.

Physical events clearly affect mental states, and schizophrenia may predispose to episodes of delusion, rage, etc. But mental dispositions *aren't causes.* They may indicate the likelihood of certain characteristic behavior, based on group sampling, but don't tell us how any given *individual* will behave in *specific circumstances.*

The golf-ball size tumor in the gun killing example may have predisposed the perpetrator to violence; and at the moment he pulled the trigger, such influence may well have become overwhelming. But this hardly rules out the perpetrator's exercise of free will during the less-eventful 45 years of his life prior to the trigger pull.

Extreme behavior induced by extraordinary influence offers no paradigm for the genesis of behavior under ordinary conditions.

Such circumstances say nothing about the capacity for free will in the absence of such influence. Nor more so than the influence of anesthesia or a mighty conk on the head.

What's Happening on the Sidelines?

Extraordinary events are few and far between.

What about the countless actions surrounding such events – the instrumental, incidental, and sideline activities surrounding extraordinary behavior? Why would influence from golf-ball size tumors, or other sources of mental impairment, preclude the exercise of choice with respect to surrounding behavior?

No evidence is offered that they do.

Harris' gun killing example (and similar tales singling out extreme conduct) focus on the main event. The dynamics involved in the surrounding conduct is never considered. Why would tumor influence dictate the specifics involved in the killing – identity of victim, choice of means, music the killer played on his way to the crime scene, etc.? Did the tumor which induced the killing cause the killer to renew his Amazon Prime membership upon his return home later that night?

The absence of free will in moments of extraordinary duress says nothing about whether free will was operative in immediately surrounding moments both before and after such duress.

It begs the question to selectively isolate moments of extreme mental debilitation from the surrounding mosaic of ordinary behavior.

Part Five: The Bodily Platform

There's no disputing the impact which neural activity has on consciousness. Prick a brain section, take some LSD, or eat a dozen Snickers bars in three minutes. No surprise, your behavior is likely to be affected. None of this precludes free will or is incompatible with human choice.

Harris suggests otherwise, arguing against free will on the basis that we are governed by bodily processes:

> *At this moment, you are making countless decisions countless unconscious "decisions" — but these are not events for which you are responsible. Are you producing red blood cells and digestive enzymes at this moment? Your body is doing these things, of course, but if it quote decided to do otherwise, you would be the victim of these changes, rather than their cause. Do you feel identical to them? If they misbehave, are you morally responsible? (p. 23)*

The reduction of human beings to bodily functions follows from the absolutist conception of free will. As a result, the ability to choose requires we have conscious control over such things as the production of red blood cells and digestive enzymes. Such claims appear no less absurd than the notion that free will requires complete control over all factors in the cosmos that would otherwise determine how we behave.

The free will paradigm embraces a more modest conception of choice. Bodily activities are part of a biological platform which permits consciousness to operate. No free will advocate would deny the profound influence of neural activity and bodily functions. The question is whether we're looking at bodily influences which facilitate life and consciousness, or bodily commands which preclude volition.

Nothing in Sapolsky's science findings precludes the capacity for choice. They suggest what common sense takes for granted – that operating through a bodily platform requires being subject to bodily influence. They suggest that conscious activities play a critical role in the operation of higher-level neural activity, which are informed by and depend upon such *non-physical* factors as meaning, interpretation, values, and judgement – none of which are to be found in the laws of physics.

This offers a profound challenge to determinist premises: without meaning and conceptual framing, such neural activity would not otherwise comprehend exactly what it's supposed to be responding to.

Part Six: It's Not About Math

According to Sapolsky, it isn't necessary to isolate every causal factor involved in human behavior in order to reasonably infer that *all* behavior is determined.

It's a matter of math. We can add up all the data from every field of scientific inquiry and confidently conclude that we're biochemical machines doing whatever our causal programming demands.

Put all the scientific results together... and there's no room for free will. These disciplines collectively negate free will because they are all interlinked... (p. 8)

Deriving metaphysical conclusions based on addition – aggregating data from sundry fields of sciences – is a perilous proposition. Add up all the 75%'s this way, the 65%'s trending that way, and the 70%'s leaning the other way, and what have you got? Outside the determinist lens, you have one long, ragtag laundry list of *influences*, based on *group averages* from d*iverse individual responses* in *artificial circumstances*, bound together by broad speculative theorizing about relevance, weight, and interpretation. None of this provides an iota of evidence as to how any given individual will behave in any defined set of circumstances.

You can buy all the Toyotas you can afford. Add them up, and you still don't have a Ferrari.

Gathering up sundry strands of scientific data doesn't allow for the inferences Sapolsky wishes to make because too many open questions lie at the root of them. A different kind of math, consistent with the state of human knowledge, was suggested in the intro:

The concept of causation is problematic. What constitutes matter is subject to speculation. Consciousness is an unsolved mystery. The relationship between mental and physical events is unknown. The foundational laws of physics don't concern causation. Physicists haven't ruled out free will or endorsed determinism. Whether the universe is deterministic or probabilistic isn't known. The extent to which micro-level determinism would require the macro level to follow suit is an open question. We don't know how life arose from matter, or how consciousness arose amidst life.

Adding up the variables in *this* math yields a different result: the combined fruits of science haven't yet resolved the fundamental cosmic questions on whose answers *the free will question depends*.

With such foundational issues pending, exactly what "scientific results" does Sapolsky think can be cobbled together to preclude free will?

Part Seven: The Missing Meaning

By determinist terms, meaning, intentions, purposes, and values are passive causal effects generated by the activity of physical forces. Experience is reducible to the predetermined activity of causal events.

But what are these physical forces?

They don't think, they don't feel, they don't reason. They have no conception of meaning or truth. They operate by force of mechanical action and behave according to causal antecedents.

The most remarkable consequence of determinist doctrine is the reduction of meaning, significance, and conceptual understanding to the dictates of physical force. What things mean and signify are whatever we're *caused to believe* they do. How concepts relate to each other is whatever *we're caused to believe* about their relationship.

Hence the most unfathomable consequence of determinist doctrine: *Physical events without any conception of meaning or significance are constantly generating complex interlocking networks of meaning and significance.*

Why would unthinkingly physical events be arranging themselves into patterns organized by meaning and conceptual principles? How could a swarm of elementary particles manage to organize themselves in a manner that generates abstract frameworks based on *non-physical, conceptual principles* – language, logic, syntax, social convention, etc.?

If mental events are truly byproducts of physical forces, then such forces *are responsible* for creating airplanes, football fields, and the collected works of Shakespeare.

Unthinking events are generating thinking….

Determinists might suggest the answer lies with evolution. After all, cognitive operations were selected over the course of evolution for adaptive advantage. They are mechanical survival skills, nothing more. The response doesn't work. It violates determinist doctrine. Thoughts, intentions, and mental experience are causal byproducts of physical forces. They are generated by extrinsic forces following physical laws. They don't influence anything.

> *Thoughts and intentions emerge from background causes of which we are unaware and over which we exert no conscious control. (p. 5)*

> *We are nothing more than we are nothing more or less than the cumulative biological and environmental luck, over which we had no control, that has brought us to any moment. (Sapolsky, p. 4)*

If experience is compelled by causal force, meaning and concepts are superfluous. The physical activity that generates them is what's governing how reality unfolds. Physical events following the laws of physics are running the causal show. The question thus remains – how and why would mechanical interactions among physical elements be arranging themselves into conceptual patterns that follow non-physical principles when physical events alone are what's governing the universe?

Social Convention and Symbolic Significance

The question becomes more puzzling when it comes to social convention. At the cognitive level, reality organizes in patterns based on meaning of significance, in which abstract purposes (e.g., commerce) employ symbolic means (e.g., money) in furtherance of social exchange (i.e., convention).

> *Physically, fiat money is just coins or pieces of paper with patterned marks on them. The effectiveness of money, which can cause physical changes in the world, is based on social agreements. These are abstract entities arising from social interaction.* [2]

Sapolsky's science findings make no sense without conceptual framing – his descriptions of neural activity hide their dependency on self-contained conceptual lattice-works of interconnected principles that follow constraints of meaning, significance, and values.

Without them, how could the PFC command the amygdala to back off and give it a rest – thus inducing you to believe "you're not that kind of person" and that the conduct you're tempted to indulge in is "bad"?

Where is the PFC getting the values by which to judge what's "good" and "bad" in the first place? What is the basis for the PFC operating under moral constraints that, depending on conditions, construe something "bad" or "good" in order to react accordingly? Where did its moral perspective come from? Dendrites and axions?

> *We might be able to tell a story about stretching without needing an elaborate story about coordination and cooperation norms…as opposed to bidding on a Rembrandt, where there's not going to be a story that doesn't involve a story about social practices.*[3]

Why would neural brain activity be triggered by a stock market crash? How did it create the stock market in the first place? Without influence from such non-physical factors as meaning and significance, it's curious that biological mechanisms would know enough about stock market movements to craft appropriate responses to the ups and downs of the Dow Jones or S&P 500.

Social relations are likewise driven by meaning, significance, and cultural values. Without such non-physical factors, they are inexplicable:

> *Roles are developed by…a combination of bottom-up and top-down interactions. Values relating to ethics, aesthetics and meaning…are a set of abstract principles that are causally effective in the real physical world…[and] crucially determine what happens. Wars will be waged or not depending on ethical stances…our values [have] crucial effects [as] irreducible higher-level entities: there is no way they can result from…r-level variables.*[4]

Absent the influence of meaning and context, it's hard to explain the momentous leap of neural excitation when, standing before a long table of funny colored numbers in Vegas, you see that tiny metal ball pop into a narrow slot on a spinning wheel. Did the amygdala place the chips down on red?

How did it know which slot calls for celebration, and which for commiseration?

———

Biological mechanics say nothing in themselves about the free will question. The issue is about how to *interpret* such processes:

Representational activity is part of the physical world and is connected with other things in the landscape. Every physical act is going to register at the representational level, and every representational act is happening in the physical world. Intelligent activity is part of physics. It moves earth and it builds cities. It hacks natural processes...altering the physical environment and the very ecology of the world. [5]

Human behavior doesn't make sense without a framework based on meaning, significance, values, and conceptual principles – none of which are found in the laws of physics. The case for neural determinism can't be made by circular descriptions which presume that non-physical, conceptual frameworks are the handiwork of blind, unthinking physical events.

But let's not quibble. If money is reducible to mere physical activity in the brain...could I have a loan?

It's okay with me if your amygdala wants to run a credit check first....

Part Eight: Conclusion

The free will question concerns the genesis of human behavior in concrete circumstances. In the free will paradigm, trends, tendencies, and group behavioral averages *reflect individual choices* operating within the boundaries and constraints of influence

– including biology, environment, culture, commonality of circumstance, and shared values.

None of the statistical observations presented by Sapolsky or Harris, or the facts on which they are based, demonstrate that individual behavior in concrete circumstances is dictated by causal events. No evidence can be found which demonstrates:

- That neural, hormonal, and other biochemical mechanisms, in conjunction with environment, alone and always are in charge of the cosmic show.

- That neural and biochemical activity could function without being influenced by intentions, purposes, values, and the assignment of meaning and significance which they generate – i.e., how neural networks could know *what* they are *supposed to be reacting to* without input that's been shaped by meaning, interpretation and values, none of which are recognized by the laws of physics.

- That trends, tendencies, and statistical averages based on group behavior don't, to a greater or lesser degree, reflect an agglomeration of individual choices made within the constraints of the influences, biological and otherwise, which serve to limit and constrain human behavior from cradle to grave.

Being born into poverty and burdened by a gene which predisposes one to alcoholism in 70% of those who had fishbowl tanks in their living room while growing up....

Such things don't preclude you from rising above adversity and becoming the next Bill Gates.

You'll likely have to settle for a tract home in the suburbs and a used Volvo. But not because it was determined that things would end up that way.

Chapter Three
THE MYTH OF CAUSATION

THE HEADLINES

Determinists attribute all human behavior to impersonal causal forces. These include subatomic activity, biology/environment, birth circumstances/upbringing, and a chain of physical states of the universe that began with the Big Bang. The fundamental premise behind all such causal sources is ignored in determinist advocacy - the problematic nature of causation, determinism's number one premise. The meaning and existence of causation is subject to scientific and philosophical contention. Harris and Sapolsky bypass the unresolved conceptual and scientific issues surrounding determinism's chief premise, presuming them irrelevant or trivial in significance. They are neither.

Part One: The World is a Machine

Determinism is based on the concept of causation.

It presumes causation exists and that its bona fides are have been established. They haven't. The nature and existence of causation is under scientific and philosophical contention.

No theory is more credible than its premises. Hence the initial problem with determinist doctrine: its advocates take its chief premise for granted, without need of critical scrutiny. Determinism rests on a foundation that hasn't yet passed inspection.

Harris and Sapolsky don't mention the issues surrounding the notion of causation or seek to consider the scientific and philosophical concerns about its nature and existence. Consistent with popular determinist advocacy, they confidently declare the case closed, proclaiming:

> *We know that determinism, in every way relevant to human behavior, is true. Unconscious neural events determine our thoughts and actions... (p. 16)*

> *Your thoughts, intentions, and subsequent actions... are the product of prior events you had absolutely no hand in creating. (p. 19)*

> *What I will do next... is fully determined by the prior state of the universe and the laws of nature.... (p. 40)*

We are nothing more or less than the cumulative biological and environmental luck, over which we had no control, that has brought us to any moment.[1]

In a remarkable reversal, the burden is thus placed on free will advocates to prove the existence of choice – to justify its premises, inferences, and conclusions.

By contrast, the notion of causation gets a free pass. This chapter is about why that isn't warranted.

Physicists of all stripes concede the laws of physics are incomplete. Whether or not free will exists is an open scientific question. Notwithstanding determinist advocacy, science *hasn't ruled out* the possibility.

Determinism's number one premise, the existence of causal relations, has a troubled scientific and philosophical history. After two millennia of debate, it remains on shaky scientific and conceptual grounds. Determinist advocacy assumes its bona fides have been established. In so doing, it presumes to know the answer to open cosmic questions whose resolution is beyond the reach of current knowledge.

Scientific challenges to the notion of causation include the following:

- *The fundamental laws of physics don't include causation.*

- *The foundation for the appearance of causal structures in a universe governed by non-causal laws is unknown.*

- *Whether the universe is deterministic or probabilistic is an open scientific question.*

- *The operation of causation is barred from key macro cosmic events under relativity theory.*

- *The operation of causation is barred from key micro-level events under quantum mechanics.*

- *The nature of matter, the medium through which causation would operate, is presently unknown.*

- *The relationship between micro and macro levels of reality is a matter of speculation - including whether micro level determinism would require the same at the macro level.*

- *Whether causation is scientifically relevant has been under dispute for more than a century.*

On the conceptual front, the notion of causation faces the following challenges:

- *The existence of causation cannot be derived from sense experience (Hume's challenge).*

- *The extent to which causation may be the product of how the human mind is structured isn't known (Kant's challenge).*

- *A half-dozen contemporary causal theories dispute the meaning of causation and the nature of its existence.*

- *No causal theory is capable of fully describing the mechanics of causation, even under ordinary conditions.*

- *The reduction of reality to physical causes can't explain why physical events organize themselves by rules of meaning, reason, language, logic, and other non-physical elements not found in the laws of physics, and without which human behavior (including the movement of subatomic particles involved in that behavior) can't be explained.*

This is the scientific and philosophical backdrop – the big picture context in which the free will question is being asked and considered. While central to the debate, these issues are largely ignored in popular discourse.

This takes off the table one of the more sensible answers, consistent with state of science and human knowledge – that we *simply might not know enough* at present to answer the free will question.

Part Two: Conceptual Problems

It's easy to take causation for granted.

We look about and see connections everywhere. One thing follows another with seeming necessity. We rely on causal relations for practical purposes, and take the existence of causation for granted. But what makes us think that anything is connected by some sort of invisible causal glue?

The meaning of causation has been disputed throughout the ages. After two thousand years of dialogue, nobody agrees on what we're talking about.

Causation is the skeleton in determinism's closet.

From Plato to Newton[2]

A sampling of definitions from some of the great thinkers of the ages:

- **Plato**: That which that "causes properties to exist" in other things.[3]

- **Aristotle**: The "primary source of change".

- **The Stoics**: The regularity and necessity which "binds events to one another".

- **Thomas Aquinas**: "Natural necessity" toward an end based on something's "power of the form", under divine purpose.

- **Descartes**: "Laws of nature" which govern the "movement of parts" in the natural world, as decreed by God.

- **Hobbes**: Motion between bodies, the "aggregate of accidents requisite for the production of the effect".

- **Spinoza**: Logical necessity, the "connection of ideas".

- **Leibniz**: The end state, or "substantial form", that follows something's unique purpose towards a final cause.

- **Locke:** The force of power in specific circumstances.

- **Mill**: The "antecedent" to which something is "invariably and unconditionally consequent".

Naturally, definitional uncertainties don't necessarily preclude existence. But conceptual problems are the starting point for any critique of determinist premises. We need to know what we're talking about before considering whether something exists, in what form it may exist, and what its existence might mean.

What do the more prominent schools of contemporary thought have to say about the nature of causation?

Regularity Theory
Hume's conception of causation is endorsed and causation reduced to regular appearance, or constant conjunction, among contiguous events. We see regular patterns, report upon their appearance, and catalogue their conditions, and that's that.

Counter-Factual Theory

The yardstick for causal relations is whether, had a given event *not occurred*, a subsequent event nevertheless *would have*. If I'd not gorged myself on hot fudge, would I have gained weight (all other things being equal)? If my girth wouldn't have widened absent the splurge, it was the cause of my weight gain.

Singular Theory

Favored by philosopher John Locke, causation is defined as the local transfer of force between specific events. Events are constantly conjoined by a concrete causal exchange – the locomotive behind all regularity of appearances.

Interventionist Theory

An event is causally attributable to an event if a possible intervention affecting the event would change or prevent the effect from occurring. If lowering taxes is followed by an increase in economic output (all other things being equal), then the tax relief causes the economic uptick. Interventionist theory is often considered a cousin of counterfactual explanation, and often used in combo.

Probabilistic Theories

An attempt to reconcile causation with quantum mechanics, such theories maintain that something (events, systems, informational networks, etc.) is a cause if it appreciably increases the probability that something else will follow.

Each theory has its problems, inconsistencies, and shortcomings. Determinism's chief premise is uncertain and controversial:

> *If we can agree on what you say when you say there's a causal connection, then we can understand what is the physics behind it. But it turns into a complete morass because people can't agree on what the right analysis of causal notions is. So people in philosophical literature are trading intuitions about increasingly artificial hypothetical cases. Someone gives a causal analysis of a causal notion someone proposes a counterexample...*[4]

A spirited battle is underway amongst contemporary causal theories.[5] Challenges to the current crop of theories bear such fanciful names as *overdetermination, unrepeatability, preemption, backtracking, ancestry, asymmetry, context sensitivity, normality, omissions, variable values,* and *impossible worlds,* amongst others.

At the end of the day, no present causal theory is capable of accurately describing the nature of causation, not even under *ordinary circumstances.*

A conceptual cloud of skepticism hovers over any definitive declaration that causation governs the universe and human behavior predestined.

Part Three: Philosophical Problems

Long before contemporary science came along to overturn Newtonian presumptions (see Chapter Four), serious challenges to the notion of causation were mounted by a triumvirate of philosophers: David Hume, Immanuel Kant, and Bertrand Russell.

Their objections are central to the debate about determinism's chief premise. They remain springboards for contemporary theorizing about causation, in academic circles and otherwise.

Hume's Challenge

Alfred North Whitehead famously remarked that philosophy is a series of footnotes to Plato.

It may be said with equal confidence that all theories of causation are footnotes to David Hume. Serious philosophical discussions regarding causal relations begin with Hume and don't get much further.

The famous argument by which he objected to the common notion of causation runs as follows:

We are never able, in a single instance, to discover any power or necessary connection, any quality which binds the effect to the cause... we only find that the one does actually in fact follow the other.[6]

There is nothing in a number of instances ... except only that after a repetition of similar instances the mind is carried by habit ... to expect its usual attendant and to believe that it will exist.

Causation is [the] sentiment or impression from which we form the idea of power and necessary connection.

In short, causation doesn't appear to reside in the objective world. It's not a fundamental feature of the universe. It's an expectation, a "feeling in the mind" that certain previously observed sequences will recur, and nothing more. It's a "customary transition of the imagination".
It's no more than a *subjective belief.*[7]
There's nobody behind the causal curtain.

Kant's Reply

Kant came along in the wake of Hume and further challenged determinism's chief premise.

He agreed with Hume that causation isn't an objective component of reality. But it was more than mere subjective "expectation". It's the product of how the human mind is structured — a combination of raw sense data and how we're set up to process that information. The human mind uses cognitive *categories* to shape sensory information into comprehensible form.

Causation is one of a dozen preconditions to human experience. What we experience doesn't reflect objective events in a world independent of mind – the categories shape how we experience reality and serve to make such experience possible. Other categories that serve as preconditions to experience include Quantity, Quality, and Relations.

The takeaway from Kant isn't whether he was correct about his categories. The broader question he pointed to is whether, and to what extent, our experience of the world is shaped by the human mind and its constitution, biological and otherwise.

Determinism presumes causation is an objective feature of the universe – a fundamental constituent of reality independent of human experience. Kant and Hume remind us there's good reason to question that assumption.

The fact that their objections remain central to contemporary debate over causation attests to their relevance in making the case against free will on the basis that causation governs the universe.

Under Hume and Kant's influence, causation took a historical turn towards the subjective.

They paved the way for the past century's rash of relativist movements, which in one way or another reject the notion of objective reality and truth – including post-modernism, structuralism, and deconstructionism

According to such ideologies, truth is a means of manipulation or gaining power. Morality is relative to the beholder. And appraising other cultures by our standards is presumptuous.

Who are we to know anything, or judge anyone?

It's safe to say that Kant and Hume would have categorically shuddered at such notions....

Part Four: Causation and The Laws of Physics

We assume science is based on causation. We assume it's about finding causal relations among contiguous events.

Neither is the case. The fundamental laws of physics don't concern cause-effect relations:

> *Dynamical laws – that is to say, laws that relate to the state of a system – are constraints on the relationships between states at different times, but there is nothing in the law itself... to say that either determines the other. We can use the laws to calculate the past state if we know the future or the future if we know the past. The direction in which information and influence run comes from*

> *asymmetries that we impose on the situation. But the equations themselves are neutral.*[8]

What runs forwards in time can run backwards – and eventually will, given enough time. To the extent the laws of physics may be deterministic (see Chapter Six), they don't support a forward directed "arrow of time" on which cause-effect relations can be based.[9]

> *It can seem like the macroscopic world is just a shadow cast by the microscopic order that unfolds with unflinching necessity. But that is not what the laws of physics suggests. There is no intrinsic order of determination at the macroscopic level. There is no pushing or "production" or control.*[10]

Hence the foundational laws of physics don't support determinist claims that human behavior is the causal byproduct of biology, environment, personal history, etc. Causation doesn't appear to be a fundamental feature of the universe.

Popular determinist advocacy repeatedly claims otherwise – that that science supports determinism and that "going against determinism is going against science". Nevertheless, the fundamental laws of nature don't validate determinist doctrine or rule out the possibility of free will.

Part Five: Lack of Scientific Relevance

Bertrand Russell sought to correct popular misconceptions about such matters over a century ago.

In 1912, he published a famous article "On the Notion of Cause", which spared no mercy in repudiating the notion of causation. He famously declared causal law:

A relic of a bygone age, surviving, like the monarchy, only because it is erroneously supposed to do no harm.[11]

Russell rejected the relevance of causation in the advanced sciences. As with Hume, he maintained that the objective existence of causation is based on an erroneous assumption about the nature of reality:

The recurrence of regularly observed sequences is no more than probable, whereas the relation of cause and effect was supposed to be necessary... [causal sequences] may at any moment be falsified.

...There is nothing that can be called a cause...or effect. [Science has replaced] same cause, same effect with sameness of relations...or sameness of differential equations.

Russell's take on the fundamental laws of physics is widely accepted in contemporary thought.

> *The concepts of cause and effect are not the fundamental concepts of our science and that science is not governed by a law or principle of causality.*[12]

Referring to Russell's "ancient relic" quote, physicist and cosmologist Sean Carroll explains as follows:

> *Many people would be surprised to hear the news that science has done away with the principle of cause and effect. It's actually true. It is not a fundamental principle of how reality works. It's a very useful, helpful way of thinking about things at a macroscopic level of reality... but is nowhere to be found in the fundamental laws of physics. We have left that behind. The fundamental rules of nature, under our best scientific understanding, don't work that way.*[13]

Where does that leave causation?
It doesn't. It's status is uncertain. The emergence of causal structures in a universe whose fundamental laws are dynamical laws of motion is an unresolved scientific mystery.

One might think this relevant to appraising the attempt to discredit free will based on a causal narrative of the universe. Neither Harris nor Sapolsky mention the ongoing search to find a scientific basis for causal structures and causation. [14]

Part Six: What's the Matter?

Causation needs something to work upon. That something is called *matter*. It's the "stuff" which determinists claim is subject to causal governance.

The problem for determinist doctrine is that science doesn't know *what matter is*. It doesn't understand what causation is supposed to be working through and governing:

What is matter? There are today no definitive answers...There is not even a consensus about what the answer should look like.[15]

The concept of matter as we understand it in daily life just dissolves away...when we peer closely.[16]

If you say what is going on, what is the physical stuff that is changing... we don't agree. Different people have different ideas about what the answer might be.[17]

While determinist advocacy confidently asserts causation governs the universe, the fundamental composition of that universe is *"the biggest outstanding mystery"* in physics:

> *There are several known notorious and outstanding mysteries about nature that beg for an explanation. These include two cosmological conundrums . A., the dominant form of mass that appears to govern the dynamics of galaxies...cannot be composed of the same fundamental constituents that make up visible matter ... and most likely made-up of some new form of elementary particle; and B., the even stranger fact [is] that the dominant form of energy in the universe doesn't seem to correspond to any matter at all... [it] appears to reside in empty space itself and this has completely defied any attempts to understand it today. It is perhaps the biggest outstanding mystery in cosmology and fundamental physics.*[18]

Causation's scientific pedigree suffered a serious setback under contemporary laws of physics. If causation is indeed driving the universe, nobody seems to know what kind of car's on the road.

Relativity theory and quantum mechanics entered the stage in the early 1900's. Relativity theory was fully developed in 1915, and quantum science by the mid to late 1920's.

As they developed, prior Newtonian conceptions about matter were jettisoned; a host of new, unresolved issues arose concerning its nature and existence.

Among the more prominent problems which remain unresolved:

Wave, Particle, or What

Science doesn't know whether matter consists of waves, particles, strings, quantum fields, some of the above, none of the above, or something altogether different. In the quantum narrative, matter evolves in deterministic fashion, but when observed appears as particles (see next Chapter). Which is it? Will string theory or some other approach find a grand unified theory which subsumes them both?

Something From Nothing

Space is permeated by "quantum fields" in which virtual particles pop into existence out of empty space, instantly annihilate themselves, and pop right back out of existence into empty space.[19] When resting at zero-point energy, *nothing physical* seems there. Is the universe comprised of physical stuff, or something else? Is matter mere potential?

The Missing Matter

Dark matter and energy are thought to constitute 95% of the known matter in universe. Assuming they exist, their behavior is unlike that of any other known element. They are generally held responsible for the universe's exponential expansion, but the matter is unsettled and competing theories, such as negative gravity, suggest otherwise. Many consider the dark twins mere placeholders – fanciful names for a problem for which there's presently no answer.

Incomplete Standard Model

The "Standard Model" is the list of all elementary particles in the universe. While often celebrated as "complete", many unresolved questions suggest otherwise, including the nature and scale of fundamental forces; whether and how such forces might be unified; whether dark matter and energy (i.e., 95% of the known universe) are included amongst what's listed; and over a dozen inconsistent or conflicting parameters among the various elements.

What's Higgs Got To Do With It?

The last known particle added to the "Standard Model" of elementary particles was the Higgs boson. The universe is filled with a Higgs field and as massless particles pass through and interact with the field, they obtain their mass, which is a function of how they react to the field. What is a particle before it has mass? Is this similar to the sound made by one hand clapping?

Relativity-Quantum Conflict

The two most successful scientific theories in history tell fundamentally different stories about the nature of reality. Relativity theory is deterministic, at least within a "light cone" (see Chapter Four). Quantum theory construes matter as deterministic and/or probabilistic, depending on theory (see Chapter Four). Whatever it may be, relativity and quantum science conflict in predictions about how matter behaves.

The unknown nature of matter is of no small consequence in evaluating the merits of determinist doctrine. The nature, existence, scope, and mechanics of causation can't be known without knowing what it's supposed to be governing. The central premise on which determinism is based will remain subject to speculation until such answers are known.

Popular determinist advocacy isn't concerned with the issues involving matter, the bulwark of causal relations on which determinist doctrine is based. Neither Harris nor Sapolsky deal with the issue.

Nevertheless, when it comes to the free will question, the unknown nature of matter is a serious matter.

Part Seven: Conclusion

No theory is more solid than its premises.

Those who propose a theory must justify the premises on which it's based – not take them for granted as givens.

Determinism rests on the notion of causation, which is scientifically and conceptually problematic. The lack of troubleshooting of determinist premises doesn't help the case against free will.

Harris and Sapolsky presume causation a conceptually clear notion whose meaning is established and understood. They presume that its existence has been scientifically tested and verified. They presume that the nature of matter is known and the operation of causal mechanics understood. And they presume causation a fundamental attribute of the universe under the laws of physics.

None of this is the case. The present state of human knowledge isn't capable of affirming determinist premises nor discrediting the existence of free will. In short, determinism presumes to know *what isn't known.*

Breezing past questions concerning the validity of its renders everything built atop them suspect and unreliable. First things first. Foremost, that means establishing the meaning and existence of causal relations.

Without addressing such matters, there isn't just cause for the case against free will based on predetermination.

Chapter Four
WHAT THE SCIENCE SAYS

THE HEADLINES

Determinists claim that science rules out free will; that it's not part of the natural order. Contemporary developments in physics is trending otherwise, having removed critical Newtonian barriers to free will's existence. Quantum indeterminacy has placed the notion of a cosmic causal chain in doubt. Relativity theory and quantum mechanics bar causation from fundamental cosmic events. Quantum non-locality violates the Newtonian notion of causation, offering the prospect of influence or connections amongst events which don't require the physical transfer of energy or any physical medium. Sapolsky and Harris selectively marshal the forces of science against free will while failing to address opposing scientific considerations and ignoring the big picture.

Part One: Contemporary Scientific Fronts Against Causation

Forget the conceptual doubts about causation.

Suppose, for argument's sake, that a coherent form of causal theory had been achieved and that the concerns raised by Hume, Kant, and Russell had been sufficiently dispelled. Contemporary physics has done more to undermine determinism's number one premise than merely throwing into question the nature of matter, what causation would be governing.

Relativity theory and quantum mechanics opened up two new fronts in the war against causation. They raised new doubts about its existence and removed significant Newtonian impediments that formerly served to bar free will's existence. As a consequence, the possibility of free will gained a degree of scientific plausibility that it hadn't previously enjoyed.

Quantum Indeterminacy

Quantum science suggests the universe may be comprised, in whole or part, by random events whose outcomes *aren't* due to prior conditions. Whether such events appear that way due to our ignorance of underlying causes is subject to contention, but traditional quantum theory accepts the existence of *true* randomness.

The entities described by quantum mechanics are very different in many respects from the substantive reality of our experience. They are both indeterminate, consisting at least in part of superposed potentialities, quantifiable probabilities for observable properties.....[1]

Those theories which reject quantum indeterminism have problems accounting for why reality manifests in probabilistic fashion and why probabilistic equations are required to explain the results of observation.[2]

The existence of a cosmic causal chain was the most significant Newtonian impediment to free will's existence. The quantum recognition of randomness cracked the causal egg: the existence of true randomness would sever the links in the causal chain and break the chokehold of the past on present.[3]

Each random outcome sends the universe spinning off in a direction that can't be accounted for by causal theory. The path the universe takes following random *event A* isn't the same path it would take had random *event B* occurred instead. No random outcome *need occur* – and nothing explains why random *event A* happened rather than random *event B*.

The recognition of randomness thus let steam out of determinism's central claim – that the universe unfolds in a predetermined succession of causal events. By all appearances, the universe is populated by random events which, within probabilistic parameters, are constantly generating novel outcomes not determined by prior conditions.

While there are questions about the extent to which subatomic randomness affects the macro-level in which we live (of which more later), the Newtonian claim that the world is predetermined is scientifically problematic.

In short, free will can no longer be barred on the basis that the past is causal prologue.

Free Will notes that randomness and uncertainty "can't make room for free will". (p. 27) Sapolsky spends more than a chapter on the problem.

From *Free Will's* chapter, *Cause and Effect*:

Chance occurrences are by definition ones for which I can claim no responsibility. And if certain of my behaviors are truly the result of chance, they should be surprising even to me. How would neurological ambushes of this kind make me free? (p. 28)

Quantum indeterminacy does nothing to make the concept of free will scientifically intelligible. And to the extent that the law of cause and effect is subject to indeterminism – quantum or otherwise –we can take no credit for what happens. (Harris, p. 30)

It was inevitable that various thinkers began to proclaim that the unpredictable, chaotic cloud... is where free will runs free. (Sapolsky, p. 64)

According to Sapolsky, free will advocates evidently argue as follows:

The idea [is] that if you start with something simple in biology and, unpredictably, out of that comes hugely complex behavior, free will just happened. (Sapolsky, p. 126)

Needless to say, nobody argues that "unpredictable, hugely complex biological" behavior is enough for free will. Nor that "neural ambushes" (which is circular determinist description) could *make us free*. Both are ludicrous claims that overstate the argument free will advocates make on the basis of such conditions. The point is that such conditions[4] would serve to break the causal chain and permit *the possibility* of free will. They aren't offered for anything more. Sapolsky and Harris devote four chapters to a pseudo-issue that can be dispensed with in two sentences by stating the *actual argument* offered by free will advocates:

71

1. *The existence of randomness, indeterminacy, etc. - for which quantum science provides credible evidence - would break the causal chain - in which case free will would not be precluded by a determined universe.*

2. *If that chain were broken, free will would nevertheless require something more - a mechanism by which consciousness could influence physical reality - which mechanism is a separate issue whose existence isn't guaranteed by mere randomness, chaos, quantum indeterminacy, etc.*

It's an equal waste of time attempting to prove that chaos is deterministic, for which Sapolsky makes a good case. Even if Sapolsky is right, the argument doesn't hold for randomness or quantum indeterminacy – each of which alone, regardless of what chaos means, is sufficient to sever the causal chain that would otherwise have precluded free will. [5]

Accusing free will advocates of using such conditions for broader purposes is itself random, if not chaotic.

Relativity Theory

Relativity theory led a separate assault against the citadel of causation. It banned its operation from the most fundamental of macro cosmic events, including the Big Bang and Black Holes.

Einstein's theory predicted that space-time becomes infinitely dense under such conditions and the laws of physics break down. The operation of causation isn't possible. [6]

Einstein wasn't gunning for causation. In fact, he was a determinist who took issue with quantum theory's probabilistic nature, [7] famously declaring that *God doesn't play dice.*

As with the recognition of randomness, however, general relativity theory raised doubts about causal dominion. Causation appears held at bay by space-time conditions. It no longer governs the universe, at least not at all times under all conditions.

Relatively speaking.

Part Two: Quantum Mechanics

Quantum science developed over the first few decades of the 20th century. The science initially arose in response to the failure of classical physics to explain certain phenomena, including:

Collapsing Atoms

Electrons circle around the nucleus of atoms in the classical model, but that would cause them to emit electromagnetic radiation. The resulting loss of energy would cause all electrons to plunge into the nucleus in something like a billionth of a second. That would mean no atoms – which would mean, no us.

Ultraviolet Catastrophe

Certain bodies absorb the full spectrum light and emit back radiation at all wavelengths. Classical science predicts the amount of light emitted is proportional to the wavelengths that were absorbed. At ultraviolet, this would cause an infinite amount of radiation. If true, your frying pan would become a supernova.

Photoelectric Effect

Electrons are released when light hits the surface of metals. Classical laws predict that lower light levels would require more time to build up the energy to pop out those electrons. The prediction was wrong – electrons are released instantly regardless of the light level bombarding them.

These and other classical misfires were solved by construing reality in terms of discrete units, or *quanta*. Subatomic activity that had previously evaded explanation under classical principles could be accounted for by postulating *incremental change*, rather than a continuous spectrum of degrees. Thus:

- Electrons orbit nuclei at certain distances and can't occupy the spaces in between – *atomic collapse problem solved.*

- Light consists of photons that can be measured in discrete packets – *photoelectric effect solved.*

- Radiation is emitted only at certain wavelengths and not anything in between – *ultraviolet catastrophe solved.*

Conceptualizing reality in terms of discrete units was a radical break from Newtonian science. It was a monumental advance in the state of science. But the new paradigm created a host of new problems, including a contradictory enigma at the heart of the universe that has never been resolved.

More than a century later, whether the world is deterministic or probabilistic remains unknown. What quantum science says about reality remains up for grabs.

Pop culture nevertheless embraced the new science's arrival with open mantra. New age gurus declared it the path to spiritual awakening.

Samsara had finally met its match.

The key to cosmic enlightenment had arrived. So did the keys to many a new shiny Cadillacs….

Fanciful new age readings of quantum discoveries challenged the imagination – but bore little or no resemblance to the science. Alas, the road to quantum liberation was paved with pop misconceptions. One might suspect they'll not last long enough to see any *new age*....

Classical physics was no longer guru in chief, to be sure – but quantum science nevertheless fails to prove we're spiritual beings. It doesn't demonstrate we go through seven levels of bardo before basking for all eternity in the radiance of quantum cosmic consciousness (presumably driving Cadillacs...).

And no – it didn't and doesn't prove free will exists.

But quantum science nevertheless challenged determinist presumptions by offering a place for indeterminacy in the universe and by the discovery of subatomic phenomena (discussed below) which refuse to follow the Newtonian causal playbook.

Twin Quantum Narratives

There's no one theory of quantum mechanics. There are more than two dozen, perhaps three. There's no official version among the contenders.

They share some common features, but are otherwise radically different. They disagree about the math. They disagree about the mechanisms at play behind quantum events. They disagree about what the science means. They disagree about...well, let's just say they disagree about everything quantum.

But each is trying to make sense of the same dilemma, the ultimate scientific mystery: there are *two conflicting narratives* about the nature of reality, each describing differing behavior and opposing properties.

On the one hand, things evolve in wave-like patterns. Knowing the state of a quantum system permits accurate prediction of future states. But the moment you look to see what's going on, no waves are anywhere to be found. Only particles, behaving as particles like to behave.

In the first narrative, the universe evolves deterministically; free will is precluded. In the second, the universe is probabilistic; the capacity for choice remains possible.

The conflict is of cosmic dimension, because waves and particles march to the beat of different drums. They have different properties and contrary behavior:

- *Waves propagate and spread out in space. They overlap and create interference in which peaks combine for strength, troughs likewise in reverse, and when the two meet cancel each other.*

- *Particles are point-like and concentrated. They don't overlap and can't create interference.*

In the Newtonian paradigm, it's one or the other. Wave, or particle. Take your choice, but you don't get both.

In quantum mechanics, all bets are off. Waves and particles seem to dance around each other and switch back and forth from one to the other with causal abandon. Physicists have been attempting to reconcile the two conflicting accounts of reality for over a century without success.

The jury is out – and nobody knows if they're ever coming back.

Double Trouble

The twin narrative problem is demonstrated by the famous *double-slit experiment*.

A stream of particles is shot at a screen with two slits. They land on a back screen that registers their landing. Straightforward enough. The results aren't. Here's what happens:

One slit open

Particles land in a clump opposite the slit they went through. Nothing surprising, there. Particles pass through the slits and hit the bull's eye on the back screen.

Two slits open

One would expect two clumps, one opposite each slit. But alternating bands of density appear instead – indicating a wave went through the slits, *not* a stream of particles.[8] Particles go in, but waves seem to come out.

Two slits monitored

When monitors are placed at the slits to track the paths the particles take, the wave pattern vanishes and two particle clumps form again. It's as if the particles know they're being watched and, in response, get bashful about being waves and land instead in particle clumps.

Single particles, hours apart

Shooting single particles at the screen, one by one, hours apart produces the same effect. Without monitoring, a wave pattern forms. If monitors are in place, it's particle clumps. Each particle seems to know whether they're being observed and goes where needed to contribute to wave pattern or clump, as the case may be. The mystery's even greater: wave patterns are created when waves pass the slits: a wave enters and two overlapping waves emerge, whose peaks and troughs cancel or enhance each other. Single particles can only go through one slit, in this case doing so hours apart. If only single particles enter a slit, no wave interference is possible. Yet somehow it happens.

Monitoring after slits

If a monitor is placed *after the slits* to observe what's going on before the back screen's hit, particles will form. If the monitor is turned off, a wave pattern will appear. In other words, observation after the slits – *after the point of no return* for wave interference to be created or not – somehow affects what went through the slits *just moments before*. Whether a wave or particles went through the slits seems to depend on a *subsequent observation*.

Erasing prior information

If a scrambling device is placed between the post-slit monitor and the back screen, particles will be observed emerging from the slits by the monitor – but if the recording of what the monitor observed is scrambled, or "erased" prior to the back screen, a wave pattern will form. The monitor *verified* that particles when through, hence no wave interreference occurred at the slits.

But lose the observational information, and the back screen reflects that a wave went through and interference was formed at the slits – the opposite of what the monitor saw. Particles in, particles out, confirmation recorded, confirmation lost, and presto – waves again!

Needless to say, none of this makes sense.

Particle streams landing as waves? Observation affecting how reality manifests? Particles observed emerging from the slits *as particles*, thereafter to morph into waves at a place where no interference can possibly occur to create a wave pattern?

> *The double slit experiment has in it the heart of quantum mechanics. In reality, it contains the only mystery.*[9]

What does any of this have to do with free will?

The biggest impediment to free will was Newtonian science, in particular its notion of causation. What happens in the double-slit experiment can't be accounted for by such causal principles. Something else is going on.

After a century of scientific head-scratching, nobody knows what.

Quantum Mysteries

The double-slit mystery opened up a whole host of related problems that remain equally unresolved. They all stem from the central problem in quantum science – what's going on when reality seemingly changes its form upon observation, referred to as the *measurement problem*.

In broad terms, the measure problem implicates the following related group of questions:

Wave-Particle Duality

As exemplified in the baffling double-slit experiment, how can reality behave like waves under certain conditions, particles under others? Is there something more fundamental behind both forms?

Wave Function

The Schrödinger equation is quantum science's central mathematical construct. It predicts the deterministic evolvement of quantum systems when unobserved. But what is it? Something physical? Or a mathematical device useful for predictions but which says nothing about reality?

Wave Function Collapse

The change from wave to particle-like behavior upon observation or measurement is called *wave function collapse*. Some quantum theories believe in it, others don't. For those that do, there are conflicting theories about what would trigger it.

Role of Observation

What role does consciousness play in the wave-particle "transition", if any? How could observation trigger the change? What kind of mechanism could be involved. What kind of observation is necessary? As Einstein famously quipped, *can a mouse change the world*?

Superposition

What are particles doing before a system is observed – are they waves, particles, or something else? The pre-observational state of a quantum system is called *superposition*. It was coined because quantum outcomes seem to suggest that particles don't occupy determinate positions prior to measurement. Many theories take superposition to mean that particles are in *all states at once* prior to measurement – as in a mystical flux of universal oneness. Other, more naturalistic views consider the quantum state to reflect the overlapping of probability distributions, not things.

Non-Locality

Pairs of particles can become entangled such that measuring one will instantly affect the other – regardless of distance, even if galaxies apart (discussed further below). How can something instantly influence something else without regard to distance, and without any means of physical communication?

Individually and collectively, such developments undermined the Newtonian notion of reality, including the presumption of causal influence between and amongst contiguous events.

Schrödinger's Cat

The Newtonian universe was determinate.

As with a cigar, a particle is a particle. It's position, velocity, and trajectory have continuity independent of human observation. Quantum science threw these notions to the wind.[10]

Irwin Schrödinger, one of the founders of quantum science, was not a fan of *superposition*. He offered his famous *Schrödinger's Cat* hypothetical in 1935 to illustrate the absurdity of the notion:[11]

Since I like cats, and the metaphor involves potential death, I'm going to substitute something more suitable, let's say a politician.

> *A politician is placed in a coffin with a poison cannister that may or may not open, depending on whether a radioactive particle inside the box decays. The odds are 50/50. Before the coffin is opened, the politician is in a superposition state - both alive and dead. Now, you might rightfully object, big deal - this is normal for politicians. But in quantum theories that endorse superposition it's literally the case. When you open the coffin, but not before then, one of the two states become determinate - and you'll know whether the politician will live, or not live, to cloud all the issues in the next election.*

Schrodinger made his point. How could particles be in multiple positions at once doing multiple inconsistent things prior to observation?

It makes sense with politicians, who'll promise anything to anyone in the same breath.

But cats?

Three proposed solutions to the twin quantum narrative problem seem to dominate current discussion. Two theories are deterministic, one probabilistic.

Pilot Wave Theory

Waves and particles are always present and work together in symbiotic fashion. Waves "pilot" the particles along their merry paths and guide them – in the case of double slit experiment, right to where they need to land to form clumps or wave bands, as the case may be. Nothing collapses because both are always present. But the question remains: why do things appear to collapse and change forms upon observation?

GRW, or Spontaneous Collapse Theory

Waves are constantly collapsing in probabilistic fashion as predicted by the theory. When we look about us we are witnessing a statistical showering of wave function collapses, endlessly occurring entirely independent of observation. But the question remains: how does it happen that enough of them collapse the instant we look at the wave function?

Many Worlds Interpretation

Waves don't collapse, but continue frolicking forward as reality splits apart and branches into millions of worlds, each manifesting one of the many probable outcomes of any observation or measurement. What we see reflects what manifested in *our world*, while millions upon millions of other outcomes spring from the same event and manifest in a different way in *countless others*.

Each theory paints a different picture about what reality is and how it works.

Their predictions are thought to be within spitting distance, but that's yet another matter subject to contention and awaits the development of more sophisticated technology.

In short, there is no official theory of quantum mechanics because nobody can agree on what it's all about. It just happens to work. That's not a bad start, but nobody knows what it says about reality.

No one theory appears to have the upper hand.

It seems all hands are stuck in *superposition*.

A Case Study – Many Worlds Interpretation

A more detailed look at the many worlds theory demonstrates the bizarre and unsettling state of current quantum speculations. It's an interpretation that could have been penned by J.K. Rowling. It probably was.

It maintains there's *no wave function collapse*. Upon measurement, waves continue forward and *every possible outcome* in every given situation actually occurs. Reality splits apart and "branches" into multiple worlds, each manifesting one of the many infinite possible outcomes. Each world is as real as the others. Say that again?

Even more frightening, there's *another you* scampering about in each world, enacting one of the infinite possible outcomes for every situation. That means billions of different *yous* are springing up into existence every moment. How often would that be? Oh, says the theory, only about *5000 times per second per individual*.

This is identity theft of cosmic proportions.

The Many Worlds interpretation is deterministic: every branch was predestined to branch out as it must since cosmic Worldfest day one. However, one wonders: if every possible outcome comes about upon every measurement…

- *Wouldn't billions of worlds be branching off in which the outcome confirms the operation of free will?*

- *Wouldn't billions of worlds be branching off in which the many-worlds interpretation is recognized as patently nutty?*

Hmmm...

But in fairness, it's not mad scientist time. The interpretation is embraced by many notable physicists. [12] In England, it's said to be the majority view.

You might be wondering by now about the guy who concocted this theory, not to mention what he might have been smoking in his pipe. It may be of no little coincidence, but its author, Hugh Everett III, is remembered by those who knew him as a rebel, practical jokester, and yes – *science fiction fanatic*....

He's now deceased, but there's no question he's laughing his head off at the number of physicists who actually take his theory seriously.

He'd have to be laughing.

At least in one universe...

Part Three: Spooky Action

The most inscrutable of quantum mysteries still remains in the wings.

Largely on the basis of this mystery, Einstein declared quantum science *incomplete* – that it had to be missing essential pieces of the puzzle.

The phenomena is called *entanglement*. Einstein himself brought it to the world's attention in a famous 1935 article, co-written with two colleagues, that questioned quantum mechanics' ability to explain reality.

Einstein famously called entanglement *spooky action at a distance.*

And he wasn't one to believe in ghosts.

Non-Local Influence

Entanglement is the ultimate quantum riddle.

Imagine having two coins. You place one under a cup on the table without looking. You flip the other and get heads. You raise the cup on the table and see tails. You spin the coin on the table and place the cup over it without looking. You flip the coin in your hand again and get tails. You raise the cup and see heads.

Every time you flip the coin, the one beneath the cup appears opposite side up. You can flip it ten trillion times, same result.[13] If you could put the coin on the table a thousand galaxies away, the same thing would happen.

Substitute particles for the coins, and you have *quantum entanglement*. There's some sort of connection between events that violate the laws of classical physics. What happens to one instantly influences its twin, even if they're galaxies apart, too far away for any manner of communication to pass between them. Doesn't matter. Measuring one affects the other instantly.

Some form of bizarre and inexplicable influence seems to be operating throughout the universe.[14]

Whatever's going on, it really *is spooky*.

Bell's Theorem and Spookiness

What does *spooky action* say about causation?

It depends on whom you ask, naturally. It's a matter of whether quantum science is comprehensive, offering a *complete* description of physical reality.

Einstein believed it wasn't – that *hidden variables* would ultimately be found to reveal the Newtonian underpinnings at play behind the quantum madness.

After his death, physicist John Bell devised a theorem that ultimately provided an answer to Einstein's suspicions.

As it turns out, Einstein was wrong. No local hidden variables of a classical nature were pulling the strings of entangled behavior. Experimental results matched the quantum predictions, proving that quantum science truly reflects how reality behaves.

A theorem formulated by John Bell and experiments conducted in the early 1980s... have shown that, where particles of matter have interacted in a certain way, the outcome of space-like separated measurements on both particles can be correlated in a way that has no explanation in terms of causal influences operating at light speed or less.[15]

Newtonian causation is out of a job, at least at the quantum level of reality.[16] While there are contrary theories (naturally), Bell's theorem suggests something extraordinary about the nature of reality:

- **Non-local influence exists.** Influence[17] needn't have any regard for distance and can jump instantly across galaxies. The universe isn't driven by "local" events.

- **Non-physical influence exists**. Influence needn't be physical, at least not in any sense currently understood. There's no physical medium or any physical communication involved in entangled influence.

Bell's theorem provided clarified the nature of quantum reality and provided evidence against centuries of Newtonian orthodoxy.

Not even special relativity theory emerged unscathed by Bell's discoveries. The ability of entangled influence to leap across galaxies violated Einstein's prohibition on anything exceeding the speed of light. Which explains why Einstein took light speed to object to it.

As it turns out, we live in a quantum universe, one that doesn't care much about prior scientific understanding.

What does this have to do with free will?

Free will advocates maintain that mental intentions influence reality. Since mental events aren't construed as physical, or not entirely physical – consciousness would need some way to "touch" physical reality to effectuate influence and intentions. Entangled influence demonstrated that such influence may exist – that certain influences don't require local physical contact.[18]

> *QM strongly suggests that the laws of nature do not uniquely determine how initial conditions change over time, but generally leave open a spectrum of possible outcomes. It thereby undermines an argument sometimes put that the physical world must be closed to non-physical affectation [by] some kind of mental force operating alongside the known physical forces.*[19]

Free will wouldn't be possible as long as influence was confined to local physical interactions among physical events. The validation of Bell's theorem removed that barrier.

Granted there's a marked difference between non-physical influence *among physical events*, and that which free will would require – non-physical influence *between mental intentions* and *physical events*.

Nevertheless, Bell's discovery validated a new form of influence without which the possibility of free will would seem to be shut out of the ballgame.

Spooky action is real, and lives to haunt another day.

Part Four: For Whom Bell's Theorem Tolls

Isn't it high time for the eulogy?

Didn't Bell's theorem unceremoniously relegate determinism's chief premise to the causal dust bin?

Not quite....

- As previously noted, there are respected physicists who dismiss spooky action and reject any such reading of Bell's theorem.[20]

- Bell's theorem doesn't rule out a non-local form of causal influence under principles yet to be discovered. The world could *still be determined*, and entangled behavior predestined – just not by the operation of local, Newtonian causation.

- Determinists argue that macro reality can still be determined even if micro reality expresses probabilistic characteristics. Sapolsky argues that micro level events can't "bubble up" to affect macro reality. Determined behavior may survive quantum weirdness. (See Chapter Six.)

In short, whether quantum science validates determinism and undermines its chief premise, causation, depends on which physicist you ask.

The probability of getting any given answer is currently unknown....

Determinists nevertheless routinely call upon "what science says" as witness in chief in its case against choice.

But science is a reluctant witness that isn't yet ready to testify. It's still trying to figure out what it's going to say when ultimately called to take the cosmic stand.[21]

> *It's extremely embarrassing, but true, that physicists don't know what to think.... The fundamental fact that we are trying to accommodate ourselves to is the fact that we have a way of describing the world that is super-duper successful, with what we call the wave function...etc. But then when we look at it, when we measure it, when we perceive or experience it, we don't see that wave function. We see a position, or momentum, or some observable quantity.[22]*

It's thus no surprise that few physicists are willing to rule out free will. Even the more skeptical concede that free will is possible:

> *If consciousness somehow plays a role in picking out one outcome...then sure, then free will might come for the ride as well. It's not definite because we don't*

fully know the laws of physics. The upshot is that the status of free will and its role within fundamental physical law remains unresolved. [23]

Hence the critical problem with arguing against free will on the basis that the world is determined:

Science hasn't yet *determined* that the world is determined....

Part Five: Conclusion

The state of contemporary physics is more uncertain and nuanced than what Harris and Sapolsky suggest. They liberally call upon science to support the contention that the world is mechanical and human behavior determined. Both claims presuppose that science has endorsed determinism. It indisputably hasn't.

The *measurement problem* is the central unanswered question at the heart of quantum mechanics. The question is whether reality unfolds deterministically under the Schrödinger equation, or whether that equation offers an incomplete description of reality requiring supplementation – either by hidden deterministic variables or by probabilistic equations reflecting the probabilistic nature of reality.

The measurement problem *is a problem* because the answer is unknown and science *hasn't* endorsed determinism.

Harris and Sapolsky proceed as if nothing in contemporary physics raised new doubts about whether the universe is mechanical or supports the possibility of free will. The reader is left uninformed of the significant scientific developments which do both. These include the exclusion of causation from significant micro- and macro-level cosmic events; unresolved problems posed by wave-particle duality; the existence of over two dozen quantum theories in conflict about whether reality is deterministic; the rejection of Newtonian causation by the experimental validation of Bell's theorem; and the existence of non-local influence operating without any apparent physical medium or mechanism.

Instead, Harris devotes three-and-a-half pages, and Sapolsky three chapters, to pursuing the straw man argument that quantum indeterminacy somehow validates the existence of free will. It doesn't. It can't. And no respectable free will advocate would suggest otherwise.

The true reason why randomness is relevant to the free will debate is obscured by attending to such pseudo-arguments – i.e., that the existence of randomness would break the Newtonian causal chain which would otherwise serve to preclude the operation of choice.

Free Will and *Determined* don't survey the relevant science respecting the free will debate. Instead, they offer *preferred interpretations* comprised of speculative resolutions to open scientific questions.

Imagine where the science of physics will be in another 100 years. How about in 500 years?

What about in 1,000?

What will be the prevailing paradigm? What will it say about the nature of reality? What will it say about free will?

It's unlikely to bear much semblance, if any, to what the current state of physics has to offer – with regard to free will or anything else. It will undoubtedly have more to say about free will than at present, which is relatively nothing.

The quantum revolution turned physics on its head in less than a century. It's hard to imagine how an even longer time frame might change the conceptual framework from which we view cosmic reality.

If history is any measure, there's very little probability that science will remain the same....

CONTENT DISCLAIMER

In view of certain content contained in the prior chapter, the author wishes to issue the following official statement of clarification:

The views and opinions expressed in this chapter are those of its author in this world only. They do not necessarily reflect the views which its author, or any other version or copy of its author, may or may not endorse in any other possible world or branched reality.

Chapter Five
THE SCIENCE OF FREE WILL

THE HEADLINES

Harris and Sapolsky call upon neuroscience studies to evidence that our brains make our decisions. The findings say nothing of the sort. They fail to find evidence of neural brain causation and provide compelling evidence *against* it. They refuse to endorse determinism and their central measurement has been discredited. After a decade of championing such findings, Harris excised all references to such studies in his recent "Best Of Harris" podcasts. A postscript nevertheless commends a single study to the listener – without noting the author's repudiation and the host of contrary findings. In all, the studies cited by Harris and Sapolsky evidence the *absence* of neural brain causation and demonstrate nothing but hype.

Part One: The Science Tests

A long line of neuroscience studies dating back to the early 1980's documents the relationship between prior neural brain activity and conscious decisions.

None of them support determinism. None of them offer evidence of neural brain causation. Even the most pro-determinist leaning findings repudiate any such notion.

Harris and Sapolsky nevertheless call upon the neuroscience studies for the proposition that our decisions are made by our brains long before we experience deciding or know what we're going to do next. The grey matter between our ears always beat us to the punch.

Harris argues that the neuroscience findings leave no room for doubt:

One fact now seems <u>indisputable</u>: Some moments before you are aware of what you will do next...your brain has already determined what you will do. (p. 9, underscore added)[1]

Sapolsky is less certain about the findings. He doesn't seem to know what to make of them, embracing two diametrically opposed positions in the pages of *Determined*. In some places he declares them irrelevant – they don't rule out free will. In others, he just as confidently declares them definitive – our brains make our decisions up to 10 seconds before we know about them.

99

Sapolsky 1.1 – Free will *isn't* threatened by the studies and survives the findings:

All that can be concluded is that in some fairly artificial circumstances, certain measures of brain function are moderately predictive of a subsequent behavior. Free will, I believe, survives. (p. 36)

The jury is still out, because the Libetian literature [main line of relevant neuroscience studies] remains almost entirely about spontaneous decisions regarding some fairly simple things. (p. 29)

...Criticisms...collectively show that rumors of Libetianism [referring to the seminal neuroscience study] killing free will are exaggerated. (page 27)

Sapolsky 2.2 – Free will *is* threatened by the findings, which rule it out:

*To hark back again to chapter 2, **the PFC is central to showing that we lack both free will** .... (p. 96)*

*We saw this in chapter 2, where way up the chain of...commands, there was **a PFC** [prefrontal cortex] **making decisions up to 10 seconds before*** *subjects first became consciously aware* *of the intent. (p. 94)*

*Thus, three different techniques…all show that at the moment when we believe that we are consciously and freely choosing to do something, the **neurological die has been cast**. That the sense of conscious intent is an irrelevant afterthought. (p. 24, bold emphases in prior quotes added)*

Sapolsky makes note of some of the key flaws in the studies, but breezes on past them to endorse their findings – at least on those occasions when he's not insisting to the contrary….

In the end, his contradictory declarations about the neuroscience don't affect his position. He believes other considerations more important:

Where did that intent come from in the first place? If you don't ask that question, you've restricted yourself to a domain of a few seconds. [It] can't start with readiness potentials or with what someone was thinking before they committed a crime. Why would you ignore what came before the present in analyzing someone's behavior?[2]

The answer is, you don't need to ignore them.

What we need is to put them in the proper perspective and not jump to the conclusion they preclude free will, rather than provide conditions that constrain its operations. Asking "where did that intent come from" presumes that its source was outside consciousness. The question presumes determinism true and the facts interpreted accordingly.

Harris, by contrast, says nothing about the well-documented flaws in the studies, including that their discredited central measurement. [3] Nor does he intimate the widespread rejection of such findings within the neuroscience community.

The Headlines, Versus the Findings

The neuroscience findings provide overwhelming evidence *against* any such causal connection. Even those cited by Harris and Sapolsky fail to find any causal connection between neural brain impulses and conscious decisions.

Why would either author suggest otherwise?

The *headlines* in the studies routinely announce groundbreaking results – highlighted in titles, subtitles, intros, double-size excerpts sprinkled about the text, etc. The actual findings they refer to are too flimsy to break much of anything, grounds or otherwise.

They routinely boast of predicting decisions: *We can predict what button will be pressed! Volitional content can be predicted!* Etc.

Great soundbites. Dramatic. But nothing to do with the findings, which don't remotely support causal relations.

The actual *predictive rates* – they don't seem to make it into the headlines. Many studies even manage to forget to put them in the main text, relegating them to the supplemental materials that you can easily locate after navigating a dozen links.

None of this explains the extent to which Harris and Sapolsky mischaracterize the findings. The *not so short* list of problems that aren't called to the reader's attention:

- *The studies refuse to endorse neural brain determinism and routinely caution any against such conclusions.[4]*

- *They report correlations insufficient for causation, often barely above chance.[5]*

- *Their central measurement has been discredited by numerous other studies for a multiple of reasons.*

- *The claimed neural mechanism for decisions is based on multi-trial averages, reflecting neural patterns which don't appear in as much as 20% of the individual subjects.*

- *An extensive body of contrary findings provide compelling evidence against neural brain causation.*

- *The studies assume the relevant sequence starts with rising neural activity, without considering the broader contextual sequence of prior conscious intentions.*

- *There's no credible evidence that wrist flicks, button presses, or other simple motor movements have any relevance to everyday decisions involving deliberation, emotional investment, complexity, future events, or non-motor movements.*

These are matters of no small significance.

Each alone is enough to halt all neuroscience arguments against free will in their predetermined tracks.

The only thing "indisputable" about the neuroscience studies is that they all *fail to demonstrate* that neural brain activity makes our decisions or determines our behavior.

Part Two: How the Studies Work

Free Will cites three studies as evidence that prior neural brain impulses call the shots – *Libet* (1983), *Haynes* (2011) and *Fried* (2011).[6]

Subjects are tasked with making a simple motor movement, a finger raise or wrist flick, while watching a timing device to note the moment they felt the urge to move. The studies use fMRI or other neural monitoring device to record two time frames: first, between the start of increased neural brain activity and the moment the subject experiences "deciding"; and second, between the experience of deciding and start of the motor movement.

Some studies track self-initiated movements, others cued responses. Some involve single hand movements, others hand selection choices. Most studies focus on pre-motor and motor cortex activity, but other brain areas have been studied.

The spontaneous urge to move a finger is presumed to arise from the same or comparable neural activity as that of a decision about where to send your child to college, which job offer to accept, or which non-FDA approved treatment one might turn to in facing a life-threatening illness.

Part Three: The Findings

The Libet Studies

Libet was the first study to explore the relationship between prior neural brain activity and conscious decisions.[7] It tracked neural activity called *readiness potential*, or RP.

It found that RP starts increasing about one-third of a second (350ms) before subjects experience deciding. The hand movement starts about one-fifth of a second after that.[8]

If free will were involved you'd expect the order reversed: conscious decision, then neural activity, then motor movement. That didn't seem to be the case. Libet thus concluded:

The brain decides to initiate or, at least, to prepare to initiate the act before there is any reportable subjective awareness that such a decision has taken place.[9]

One might ask what it means to "prepare to initiate" a decision. Does that mean the brain is doing the deciding, or that such neural activities reflect one aspect of a larger decisional process that began with the intention to participate in the study and continued through following its protocols?

No matter. Libet repudiated his initial study based on findings from subsequent experiments. He found we can always *veto* an earlier "decision" – even *after the start of* the RP activity which determinists maintain make our decisions:

The conscious will (W) does appear before the motor act, even though it follows the onset of the cerebral action (RP) by at least 400 ms. That allows it, potentially, to affect or control the final outcome of the volitional process. In a veto, the later phase of the cerebral motor processing would be blocked, so that actual activation of the motor neurons to the muscles would not occur.[10]

Harris acknowledged Libet's reversal in a footnote, while giving stage center to his earlier, repudiated findings in the main text.[11] Harris offers a one sentence commentary about Libet's reversal calling the veto "absurd", arguing it would have to "arise unconsciously as well". (p. 73) Yet if that were the case, it should be reflected in similar RP brain activity *before the veto*. Harris cited no study for any evidence of such activity. In fact, Libet's second study reported that the RP suddenly *dropped* right before the veto:

> *A substantial RP developed during the 1-2 actual seconds before the veto, in accordance with the subject's report of feeling an expectation to act. But* **this RP flattened at about 100 to 200 msec before the preset time,** *as the subject vetoed the act and no muscle response appeared. This at least demonstrated that a person could veto an expected act within 100 to 200 msec before the preset time for the act (Bold emphases added).*

This pattern of RP activity is not what one would expect were Libet's theory indeed "absurd". Harris doesn't look to the veto findings, which suggest otherwise:

> *In those voluntary actions that are not "spontaneous"... in which conscious deliberation ...precedes the act, the possibilities for conscious initiation and control <u>would not be excluded by the present evidence</u>.* [12] (Emphasis added.)

Nevertheless, Libet's 1984, initial study remains the centerpiece of determinist presentations of the neuroscience. The findings are loudly trumpeted in validation of determinist doctrine – "indisputable" evidence, says Harris, that our brains decide what we'll do next before we have a clue.

In 2005, Libet summed up the position he's maintained for over 30 years following his initial study. Given the hallowed place his first study occupies in determinist mythology, it's worthwhile to consider what he had to say:

> *The determinist materialist view is a belief system. It is not a scientific theory that has been verified by direct tests. The non-physical nature of subjective awareness...is not describable or explainable directly by the physical evidence alone.*
>
> *As a neuroscientist investigating these issues for more than 30 years, I can say that these subjective phenomena are not predictable by knowledge of neural function. This is in contrast to my earlier views as a young scientist... before I began my research on brain processes in conscious experience, at age 40.*
>
> *In fact, conscious mental phenomena are not reducible to or explicable by knowledge of nerve cell activity. Even if a structure is necessary to the conscious function, that does not, in itself, make that*

structure a sufficient condition for producing conscious experience.

Studies in neuropsychology... give us information only about where in the brain the nerve cell activities may be related to various mental functions. They do not tell us what kinds of nerve cell activities...nor sufficiently indicate the timing... between changes in nerve cell activities and a mental function.

Thus it is not possible to answer questions such as, does conscious intention proceed or follow the cerebral initiation of a voluntary act.

Finally, on the role of free will directly:

Conscious will definitely can control whether the act takes place. We may view the unconscious initiatives for voluntary actions as "bubbling up" unconsciously... the conscious will then select which of these initiates may go forward...or which ones to veto and abort so no act occurs. This kind of role for free will is actually in accord with commonly held religious and ethical structures.[13]

Libet's much touted 1984 initial study doesn't, at least in its author's view, provide *indisputable* proof of anything, other than the fact that no such proof exists.

Harris isn't alone in offering a selective history of the neuroscience. Sapolsky also mentions the Libet veto, but prefers to emphasize the views of "a young scientist" over 30 years of that scientist's conclusions to the contrary.

The Haynes Study

The second study cited by *Free Will* is *Haynes*.[14] According to the headliner, *Haynes* –

found two brain regions contain[ing] information about which button the subjects would press a full 7 to 10 seconds before the decision was consciously made. (p. 8)[15]

This sounds impressive, but what does that curious phrase, "containing information" mean? As it turns out, it refers to a *60% correlation* rate between prior neural activity and conscious decisions.

60% is barely above a coin toss.

The correlation rate doesn't evidence causation but the lack of it: a cause doesn't fail to produce its necessary effect 40% of the time under like conditions. *Haynes* conceded this was the case and warned against concluding otherwise:

*It has not been established whether early predictive signals **are decision-related at all**. (Emphasis added)* [16]

Despite Haynes' express disavowal, Harris claims it supports the *indisputable* conclusion that our brains make our decisions.

Sapolsky, by contrast, defers to a quote from Roskies in summarizing Hayne's predictive levels:

All [Haynes] suggests is that there are some physical factors that influence decision-making.[17]

An accurate headline for *Haynes* would be:

Brain activity from two regions correlates 60% of the time with a button press, such "information" demonstrating the lack of causation between such brain events and conscious decisions.

Harris is right that the Haynes study offers "indisputable" evidence – it just happens to be evidence *against* the idea that our brains make our decisions.

The Fried Studies

Fried is the third study cited by Harris[18]

The introductory headline is even more dramatic than the others:

The activity of merely 256 neurons was sufficient to predict with 80% accuracy the person's decision to move 700 milliseconds before he became aware of it. (p.80% accuracy? Only 256 neurons?

Free will's head finally seems to be on the causal chopping block. It seems there's a neural smoking gun after all. Alas, the findings aren't as advertised:

- *Data for the 80% headline stunner came from four subjects, not the full 12 in the study.[19]*

- *70% of the data came from two subjects, who had the majority of responding neurons.[20]*

- *As conceded, there was no consistency in number or placement of electrodes per subject.*

- *The 80% figure was based on neural ensembles. "Classification performance" drops to 65% when measured by averaging individual subjects and trials.[21]*

- *The study concedes there were "wide variations" in individual rates from subjects, disqualifying the data from reflecting a universal neurological process.*

- *The subjects had a neurological disease, but we're told "most" of the data wasn't from affected regions. What does "most" mean? 90%? 75%? 65%? Possible contamination was noted but never quantified.*[22]

Put all such methodological concerns aside. Harris fails to inform his readers of Fried's *actual conclusions,* which refuse to endorse neural brain determinism:

> *It remains unclear whether the emergence of volition is causally related to the neuronal changes described. The relationship between neural activity in the motor cortex and the emergence of consciousness remains a topic of debate.*[23]

Sapolsky's again quotes Roskies in summing up the Fried data:

> *While the 80% range is certainly better than chance, this sure doesn't constitute a nail in free will's coffin.*[24]

An accurate headline for the *Fried* findings would be:

A sampling of neural ensembles from inconsistently placed electrodes in four subjects found neural activity correlating 80% of the time with conscious decisions, with a 65% classification performance when averaging individual subjects and trials. The majority of data came from two subjects out of four, and some portion of data could have been contaminated by neural disease.

Perhaps ignoring the findings for the headlines could have been predicted...

Fried Hand Choice Study

Fried also did a separate hand choice study.

This time only *three subjects* were used, no explanation given. *Fried* headline is again far more dramatic than the findings. Fried claims the hand choice data:

...*allows us to predict which hand the subject will opt to use.*[25]

This sounds impressive. Isn't the prediction of hand choices a major breakthrough? Not if the predictive rate is woefully below causal levels. No surprise, the rate isn't mentioned in the headlines. It isn't even mentioned in the text. The relevant chart in the Supplemental Materials indicates a peak hand-choice predictive rate of 65%.

As with Haynes, barely above a coin toss.

Don't bet your life savings on that kind of predictive rate.

Part Four: Causes, Correlations, and Prediction

Why are the neuroscience findings so routinely misrepresented? Part of it may be that the studies are often framed in a way that promotes two misconceptions:

- *Correlation isn't evidence of causation.*

- *Prediction isn't evidence of causation.*

Causation isn't correlation – it's a *necessary connection* between events. When a cause occurs, the effect will necessarily follow under like conditions. Correlation is a *statistical correspondence*, by two or more events, which may not have any causal connection between each other. This can result from coincidence, common causes, unknown conditions, insufficient data, etc.

Did you know?

- *Divorce rates in Maine correlate with U.S. margarine sales. Both increase and decrease in similar patterns. Would you be tempted to conclude that divorces cause increases in margarine consumption, or vice versa?*

- *The consumption of mozzarella cheese correlates with civil engineering doctorates. They generally increase and decrease together. Would you conclude that the popularity of mozzarella creates a rabid interest in civil engineering, or vice versa?*

- *Ice cream sales correlate with shark attacks. Both often increase in certain locations. Would you conclude they cause each other, or that people swim more often and consume more ice-cream in hot weather?*[26]

As it is with cheese, ice cream, and sharks, so it is with causation. The neuroscience findings don't report having found *causal connections*, but rather *non-causal correlations*.

They provide no evidence that neural brain signals cause our decisions. Reports of free will's death by shark attack have been greatly exaggerated.

Predictions

The word *prediction* creates similar confusion.

It's liberally bandied about in the neuroscience headlines, bringing a dramatic flair to otherwise unremarkable or mundane findings.

But predictions refer to *correlations*, not causation.

The ability to predict something requires only that one be right more times than not. Get it right more than 50% of the time, and voila – you've *predicted something*. Congratulations! That's all it takes.

Sapolsky concedes that low predictive rates reflect correlations, not causation:

> *Something close to 100% accuracy would be a major blow to free will belief. In contrast, the closer accuracy is to chance… the less likely it is that the brain "decides" anything. As it turns out, predictability isn't all that great. In the Haynes study, fMRI images…predicted which behavior occurred with only about 60% accuracy, almost at the chance level. (Page 31)*

Haynes also cautioned against confusing correlation with causation for this very reason. It went a step further, noting that even *the highest* of correlation rates can't be assumed to signify causal relations:

Even a 100% correlation rate does not necessarily indicate causation. [27]

What, even 100% isn't enough? How could that be?

Every day I get out of bed, the Moon circles the Earth. It's the same every single day – even on national holidays! The correlation rate is 100%.

While my astrologer might disagree, the Moon's orbit doesn't cause my getting out of bed.

Nor, I suspect, does the Moon's orbit depend on my getting up.

Discredited Methodology

The most fundamental problem with the studies referenced by Harris and Sapolsky was noted in the opening introduction:

Their central measurement *has been discredited.*

The isn't opinion or speculation. The studies themselves concede the problem – the central measurement, the moment of conscious decision, *can't be accurately determined.* Subjects can only give retroactive estimates that are *inherently unreliable.*[28]

The problem arises from:

Short Time Frame

The studies measure events that are tenths of seconds apart. The Libet study reported 350ms between neural activity and decision, and 200ms between decision and movement. Try counting a third of a second silently to yourself. Try counting a fifth!

Distraction

Subjects in the tests must divide their attention among cues, mental anticipation, muscle readiness, instructions, warding off distractions, remembering the moment, etc. – all while watching a revolving timing device or flashing numbers or letters on a screen.

Distortion

Subjective estimates are highly susceptible to influence, both before and after their estimate of timing. Priming, masking, backward masking, subliminal stimuli, working memory, timing device, post-decisional cues – these are among the many documented influences that affect estimating when the conscious decision occurs. (p. 70, footnote 1)

The *Fried* study thus concedes:

Inaccuracies of several hundred milliseconds would have led to a large decrease in the number of neurons responding ... and could bring the results very close to chance.[29]

Free Will itself acknowledges the problem:

Such judgments are retroactive estimates based on the apparent time of movement and not based on the actual awareness of the neural activity. (p. 70, footnote 1)

Harris notes the inaccuracy problem to show our sense of making decisions is flawed. But it's a double-edged sword that invalidates the very findings he uses to make his case: they have no value if their central measurement is a "retroactive estimate", incapable of documenting the basis for the conclusions he's championing.

I can confidently declare what I just said is accurate. Within a few hundred milliseconds….

Interpretation

Suppose there's no timing issue or other methodological concerns. What do prior neural impulses mean?

Are they decisions, or part of a decisional process? Do they cause decisions, or are they precursive neural activity in preparation for an upcoming choice?

There is no consensus within the neuroscience community. Recent seminars about neuroscience and free will suggest the majority reject the notion that such prior neural activity cause our decisions.[30]

Other neuroscience interpretations are no less plausible and consistent with the facts if not more so, including:

- *Non-specific neural excitation as decisional commitment approaches.*

- *Preparatory activities in anticipation of a conscious decision.[31]*

- *Precommitment urges or desires which the ultimate conscious decision needn't follow.*

That prior neural signaling reflects general processes, rather than specific decisions, is endorsed by numerous neuroscientists and backed by substantial evidentiary findings.

> *The RP seems to reflect a general expectation or an unspecific motor preparation.[32]*

In the preparatory action theory, RP is construed as revving up the engines, like a runner getting into position before the whistle sounds:

> *Both RP and LRP studies appeared to be a non-specific electrophysiological sign of participation in the task, not a specific sign of covert movement preparation.[33]*

Non-causal interpretations are endorsed in multiple neuroscience studies and related literature.

Harris and Sapolsky don't mention them.

Relevance

Are the science findings relevant?

They all concern simple motor decisions. They don't involve deliberation. In Libet and similar studies, subjects are asked to note when they first feel "the urge" to move. Neuroscientists question whether these are decisions, rather than spontaneous impulses. They certainly involve no deliberation, the hallmark of conscious decision-making.

Do arbitrary motor movements have anything to say about choices in general?

Sapolsky notes that a limited number of studies have replicated Libet findings in other settings [34]. On the other hand, some haven't. But none involve choices in which there's any real investment; those which require weighing multiple factors; those which involve longer time frames than a wrist flick; those involving moral considerations; etc.

There's thus no reason to believe that any data from the Libet line of findings can be generalized beyond minor motor movements in contrived conditions. There certainly isn't any compelling evidence this is the case. Libet himself questioned the matter in the quote cited previously.

While rarely addressed by determinists trumpeting the neuroscience, the issue of relevance is highly relevant.

Selective Sequencing

Why start the sequence with neural activity?

In the *Libet* studies[35], neural brain activity kicks off the sequences that are studied. But those signals occur within a broader contextual sequence that includes prior conscious activity.

> *The most significant relevant decision by the participants, namely the decision to participate in the experiment and to push the button within a short period of time, is made before the readings of the brain activity.*[36]

But kicking the game off with neural events is a self-fulfilling prophesy that puts such activity first in line as causal instigator of what follows. Other lines of neuroscience research don't make that presumption. Starting the relevant sequence with conscious events leads to another story:

> *...recent investigations have established that one more significant way to fire the cortical neurons is just to image an action without an actual movement. There is also evidence that shifting from one mental task to another changes the pattern of brain activation.*[37]

Start with eggs and you're likely to end up with an omelet. Start with ice cream and you're likely not to.

The issue of sequencing affects the credibility of determinist conclusions based on the neuroscience findings and cannot be ignored in evaluating what such studies suggest.

Harris and Sapolsky don't address the problem.

Part Five: The Opposing Science

A prolific line of neuroscience studies rejects the idea of neural brain causation. Harris and Sapolsky invoke the authority of selective neuroscience studies without informing the reader of the numerous contrary findings.

Some of the many well-known studies that challenge the idea that our brains make our decisions:

Random Fluctuations

Random neural fluctuations appear to correlate more closely to motor movements than RP neural brain activity. According to the Schurger study:

> *Random neural fluctuations more closely correlate with Libet movements than RP activity. The level of random fluctuation occurs long after "the brain" must have decided. The brain can't have decided if*

the action depends on subsequent bodily activity unconnected with the start of RP.[38]

In light of Schurger, perhaps RP should stand for *really problematic?*

Co-Variation

John Stuart Mill noted that causally related events must *covary* with each other – when one changes, the other must change accordingly.

According to the Haggard study:

Co-variance reflects the presence of causal relations – when factors are varied for the cause, they will be reflected in the effect. Changes in RP timing... do not reflect the fundamental co-variance of causation. [This] rul[es] out the RP as a cause.... [39]

RP is the basis for most studies about pre-decisional neural activity. Haggard discredited its causal role based on the lack of co-variance: RP's that started earlier didn't coincide with early experiences of deciding.

But Haggard *did* find co-variance when tracking the LRP (RP activity on the opposite side of movement). Was this the causal link that demonstrated neural brain causation? Alas, Libet himself cast doubt upon it: Haggard compared earlier experience of when to move (RPI), not what Libet considered the more important measure, the actual "act now" experience (RPII).

> *LRP onset is not the starting point of the psychological processes that culminate in voluntary movement".*

Determinist claims about the neuroscience presume such matters resolved in favor of determinist principles. Haggard indicates the opposite, but determinist pronouncements ignore the complexities and uncertainties that haven't been resolved at the heart of these studies.

Post-RP Instructions

When subjects make a hand selection in response to a cue given *after* RP activity has started, the neural activity reads the same no matter which hand moves.

How could that be the case if a specific decision has already been made by the brain moments before?

According to the Hermann study:

> *Random cues given after RP startup told subjects which hand to move. [That] can't be known at RP startup when the brain has already decided. The measurement of RP activity doesn't change no*

matter which hand moves. Something else altogether determined the movement. RP cannot determine which of the two alternatives is executed.[40]

The study provides compelling evidence against the notion that prior neural brain activity causes subsequent decisions.
Harris and Sapolsky don't cite the study.

Decisions Not to Move

Findings demonstrate that RP activity remains the same in decisions *not to move*.
According to the Trevena study:

RP activity was the same when subjects decided to move or not upon hearing a cue given after RP had started and the brain had "decided". RP could not have caused the subsequent decision… because… [it was] unknown upon start of RP. [RP] … seems to indicate a general ongoing involvement….These results provide further evidence against…unconscious determination of our decisions.[41]

Why would the brain be stimulating neural activity for an upcoming movement that it's already decided *not to make*? Isn't this compelling evidence that no such decision was made at the time of such prior neural activity?

My brain's not coming up with any answer ...

Reaction Studies

Stop studies demonstrate that cued decisions may originate as late as 200ms before motor movement. The decision couldn't be caused by RP activity, which starts increasing 350ms before the stop decision.

According to the Schultze study:

Stop decisions in response to a cue can be implemented 200ms before the upcoming movement. This is virtually the same timeframe that Libet found between conscious decision and movement, supporting that the decision is made at the time of the conscious decision. [42]

———

These are some of many findings which provide troubling, if not compelling evidence against neural brain causation.[43]

They form an integral part of the neuroscience landscape. Sapolsky and Harris don't mention them in presenting the neuroscience findings, thus providing an inaccurate survey of the landscape.

Despite such neglect, the contrary neuroscience findings just can't be vetoed away....

Part Six: Conclusion

Scientific authority is by nature impressive. After four decades of neuroscience studies, what do the neuroscience findings amount to?

Given the frequency with which determinists call upon the authority of neuroscience studies and the degree to which they misreport the findings, it's worth recapping what the actual record demonstrates and the extent to which it provides compelling evidence against neural brain causation. In summary:

- *Across the board refusal to endorse neural brain determinism.*

- *Correlations insufficient to evidence causation, at rates demonstrating the lack of causal relations between neural activity and conscious decisions.*

- *Findings based on multi-trial averages of widely diverse individual responses, often with as many as 20% of subjects showing no sign of such neural activity.*

- *Claims of predicting choices based on predictive rates insufficient to infer causation - rates which often aren't disclosed in the headlines or main text and appear only in supplemental materials.*

- *A discredited central measurement confirmed in numerous science findings for a multiplicity of reasons - a problem acknowledged by Harris, Sapolsky, and in the studies they cite.*

- *Data pools of as little as 3 or 4 subjects, on which determinists proceed to base fundamental metaphysical truths about the nature of consciousness.*

- *Inconsistent methodologies and lack of corroboration by subsequent findings under like conditions.*[44]

- *Selective use of sequences which presume the decisional process begins with neural events and consider prior conscious activity, including the decision to participate and perform as instructed, irrelevant.*

- *No evidence that the neural architecture in simple motor movements is comparable to that of non-arbitrary, non-motor decisions, including everyday choices of greater complexity, emotional investment, non-immediate action, etc.[45]*

- *Non-causal interpretations of equal or greater plausibility with no less evidentiary support, including the construal of prior neural activity as non-specific preparatory processes.*

- *Extensive contrary findings offering compelling evidence against neural brain determinism on multiple grounds.*

In short, *no reading* of the neuroscience landscape supports the case against free will.

By calling upon the neuroscience, Sapolsky and Harris unwittingly present compelling evidence in the case *against* neural brain determinism.

But don't take my word for this.

My brain may have decided to write these words a few milliseconds before they occurred to me....

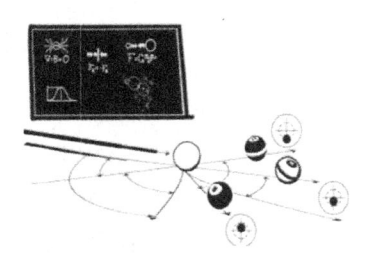

Chapter Six

VIOLATING THE LAWS OF PHYSICS

THE HEADLINES

Determinists argue that free will would violate the laws of physics. The universe unfolds in a chain of global states that started at the Big Bang. Human intervention would disrupt the natural order. This presumes science sufficiently developed to preclude the discovery of laws that would validate the capacity for choice. Yet acclaimed physicists concede that science hasn't ruled out free will. While science concedes it doesn't understand what it means to be "physical", determinists embrace a circular definition of the natural order in which only "physical events" have influence. This would undermine science itself, which is based on non-physical events such as meaning, appraisal, judgement, and theorizing.

Part One: The Natural Order

Physics can't make sense of free will. Is it thus reasonable to infer that choice doesn't exist? Harris and Sapolsky reject free will on the basis that it lacks scientific validation:

> *No one has ever described a way in which mental and physical processes could arise that would attest to the existence of such freedom. Most illusions are made of sterner stuff than this. (p. 6)*

> *Find me the neuron that started [an action]... and then we can talk about free will....*

Such claims presume science is sufficiently developed to preclude free will from the natural order. Yet acclaimed physicists and Nobel laureates refuse to rule it out. The history of science belies the notion that scientific understanding is the barometer of existence: today's lack of knowledge is tomorrow's certainty.

Determinists nevertheless endorse a definition of "natural order" which reduces everything to physical activity. The exercise of choice would be waving a magic wand over the laws of physics and causing the cosmic order to run amok. Free will would require the supernatural. Its existence would necessitate that

> *"[a] nonbiological essence of you is bespangled with fairy dust (p. 93)*

Free will advocates argue otherwise – if free will were to exist, it would be *part of* the natural order. In the absence of definitive scientific proof to the contrary, the determinist definition of "natural order" is circular:

- ***Free Will doesn't exist because it would violate the natural order.***

- ***The natural order consists of physical events following physical laws.***

Determinism presumes science has evolved to the point where it understands what it means to be *physical* and is thus in a position to know what does and doesn't belong to the natural order. Physicists concede that isn't the case:

The reality of the physical world itself seems more nebulous than it had seemed to be before the advent of the superb theories of relativity and quantum mechanics. The very precision of these theories has provided an almost abstract mathematical existence for actual physical reality.[1]

We can predict with incredible precision the probability of getting certain outcomes. But then if you ask what happened in between, we don't even know. It's not just that we don't know the math or the physics, we don't know either one.[2]

If we're really honest about it, quantum mechanics is something we don't have an answer to. We can give predictions...but we can't tell you what's really going on.[3]

There is now no more agreement about what quantum theory means than when Einstein and Bohr first debated the question in the 1920s.[4]

Anybody who thinks we're at the end of the story is misguided. We can expect a lot of surprises in the future.[5]

Anyone who claims to understand quantum physics is either lying or crazy.[6]

What constitutes the natural order is up for grabs. The most advance scientific theory of our time is unable to "tell us what's really going on". Demanding scientific attestation for free will is throwing causal stones in a glass house of scientific uncertainty.

As a matter of science, determinism is no more qualified for membership in the natural order club than the capacity for human choice.

What Did We Know 100 Years Ago?

Scientific "attestation" must be placed in context. Free will doesn't stand alone in the shadow of cosmic mystery.

Little more than a century past, scientists didn't know that atoms were made of protons and neutrons. A half century later, it turned out these weren't their fundamental constituents. When quarks were discovered, scientists had much to learn about their nature. Thanks to quantum mechanics, fundamental aspects of their behavior remain uncertain.

Below is the short list of the more notable scientific discoveries since the turn of the prior century:

- *E = MC2 (1905)*

- *The nucleus (1911)*

- *Curved space-time (1915)*

- *The proton (1919)*

- *The expanding universe (1922)*

- *Galaxies (1923)*

- *Big Bang theory (1927)*

- *The neutron (1932)*

- *Nuclear fission (1939)*

- *Cosmic radiation (2003)*

- *The Higgs Boson (2012)*

Given the mind-boggling pace of scientific discovery, acclaimed physicists are loath to conclude that anything in the current laws of physics rules free will out:

> *I could be totally wrong about [free will]. If new evidence or argumentation comes to show us that there's a better way of understanding the world and if that's the case, we will change our minds...there might be answers to all these questions.*[7]

Existence is a complicated business. What level of "attestation" is enough?

Dark matter and energy are a case in point. They are thought to constitute 95% of the matter in the universe, yet await scientific confirmation:

> *This weird dark energy which we don't understand and weird dark matter [for] which... we have no evidence... appears describe the universe. [But] anyone who tells you they have an idea about dark energy is lying ... It's the most bizarre thing in physics. It's inexplicable in a fundamental way.[8]*

One might think the regularity by which intentions match behavior no less qualified to support the provisional acceptance of human volition. Determinists presume we know what we don't based on evidence that doesn't exist:

> *Human choice or animal choice is completely unintelligible to us. We can't deny that it happens we all know perfectly well that we make choices, we make decisions. But it's not only beyond the range of existing science, no one has a coherent idea of how you can explain it. If we know something to be true but can't explain it, so much for our explanatory possibilities....[9]*

Our descendants will undoubtedly shake their heads in disbelief about what current science is capable of "attesting" to.

More than likely, they'll view the prevailing state of science as *attesting* to nothing but our ignorance.

Part Two: Cosmic Dominoes

Can free will be squared with the laws of physics?

The determinist paradigm wholeheartedly rejects the notion. We are captive to the physical state of the universe. A succession of global states going back to the Big Bang determines everything we think and do. A string of cosmic dominoes governs how the universe unfolds:

> *Each prior influence flows without a break from the effects of the influences before. There's no point in the sequence where you can insert a freedom of will that will be in that biological world, but not of it. We are the outcome of the prior seconds, minutes, decades, and geological periods before, over which we had no control. (Sapolsky, p. 46)*

The idea that the universe unfolds in a sequence of causal influences seems straightforward, but is scientifically problematic:

The Direction of Time

Cause-effect relations require that time run forward; that an *arrow of time* exists whereby causes precede effects. The fundamental laws of physics don't support such time *asymmetry*:

any sequence that runs forwards can equally run backwards – and will do so, given enough time.

Under the laws of physics, a falling egg doesn't *cause* the splatter on the floor any more than the spatter causes the egg to drop. This morning, the egg came first. Tomorrow, it may happen in reverse – the splatter may jump off the floor right back into the simmering frying pan. You might have to go to work hungry.

Under the dynamical laws of physics, both conditions – whole egg, splattered egg – are *relative states* in a dynamical relationship that works in both directions. Reality is *time-symmetric* and doesn't play temporal favorites:

> *The most fundamental laws appear in modern science as functional relations without any intrinsic direction of determination. Causal relations incorporate a temporal asymmetry that dynamical laws do not. Without an intrinsic direction of determination, we can no more say that our actions are determined by their antecedents then that their antecedents are determined by our actions.*[10]

Science doesn't know why time run forwards only. Speculation suggests such directionality may have its roots in the 2nd law of thermodynamics, which provides that entropy (disorder) tends to increase in closed systems as time runs forwards. A low entropic state at the beginning of the universe may be responsible for time's arrow. If this theory were true, it would nevertheless leave open whether forward-directed time is a necessary or contingent feature of the universe.

The fundamental laws of physics thus provide no basis for successive causal sequences in which prior events dictate what follows. In short, science can't explain the existence of causal structures. The cosmic domino narrative, in which behavior is "the product of prior events", isn't supported by science.

No Single State of the Universe

The successive global state theory has other problems. Each such state is a frozen slice of time comprised of particles, events, and processes in fixed space-time relationships with every other.

Under Einstein's general relativity theory, there's no such thing. It rejects the notion of *absolute* spacetime in which fixed coordinates exist among events giving rise global states of the universe. Event relations are relative to the *frame of reference* from which events are viewed. The order of events may be reversed depending on one's motion relative to what's being observed and other viewers. Under relativity theory:

- Moving clocks run slow. Time speeds up (or slows down) based on the frame of reference from which the observation is made.

- Two events that are simultaneous in one frame of reference may appear sequentially in another. Event A may precede event B from one frame of reference, but manifest in reverse order to another observer.

- Length, width, and dimension of an object will expand (or shrink) based on the relative speed of the observer.

In the famous twin experiment, the twin remaining on Earth ages thousands of years relative to the twin returning from a rocket excursion at near light speed.

Under relativity theory, there's *no single* state of the universe at any given point in time because there's *no single* frame of reference by which any such state could be fixed in spacetime. Without fixed spacetime coordinates, the causal narrative based on sequential cosmic states is a fiction.

It no longer makes sense to talk simply about spatial relations between any two events or the temporal relationship...because the world just doesn't divide up in such a way. Does relativity entail that what happens at some finite interval in the absolute future was determined by the absolute past? The answer is straightforwardly no, never. Strictly speaking the world does not divide... into total states that can be compared with one another at different points.[11]

Popular determinist advocacy presumes otherwise. According to Harris:

> *What I will do next, and why, remains, at bottom, a mystery – one that is <u>fully determined by the prior state of the universe</u> and the laws of nature. (Emphasis added.)*

Which prior state? Whose frame of reference? Unless Einstein was wrong, none of them match up with any other. The contents of each such "prior state of the universe" differ.[12]

Harris' and Sapolsky's claims are based on a Newtonian view of the universe that was superseded by Einstein's relativity theory over a century ago, in 1905.

There's simply *no state of the universe* in which the state-of-the-universe argument makes sense.

Random Events Versus Predetermination

Harris and Sapolsky concede the existence of true randomness, not based on ignorance of underlying causes. Such events would knock any cosmic row of dominoes off its predetermined path.

Random events break the causal chain (see Chapter Four). No random outcome need manifest in lieu of another and each such outcome sends the universe spinning off in a different direction than otherwise. Randomness switches the train tracks, directing the locomotive of the universe towards a destination that doesn't appear on the schedule.

It's either randomness or predetermination. You can have one or the other, but you don't get both.

Micro Versus Macro Reality

The cosmic domino argument presumes that successive micro-world events govern macro level reality. The matter is subject to scientific contention. To begin with, there's no clear dividing line between micro- and macro-level reality. Putting that issue aside, Sapolsky maintains that quantum effects don't "bubble up" to break the causal chain and thus support the possibility of free will. This presumes science understands how and to what extent quantum effects influence macro-level reality. It doesn't.

In the "quantum Zeno effect":

> *The determination of what measurements are to be made on a quantum system is not prescribed by the laws of QM, and that determination does affect how the system under consideration changes. Indeed, the determination of <u>when</u> measurements are to be made can substantially affect the probabilities of outcomes. For certain systems, sufficiently frequent measurements can make vanishingly small the probability of an outcome that would otherwise have substantial probability.*[13]

According to physicist Leonard Susskind:

Imagine a car parked on a hill with a dip in it. It's clear that if the car is parked at the bottom of the dip it won't suddenly start to move. If the car is initially at rest it won't have the energy to move uphill. But remember everything not forbidden is compulsory. If the car was quantum mechanical, as all cars really are, nothing would prevent it from suddenly appearing on the other side of the hump. That might be very unlikely...but it would not be impossible. thus given enough time it would be compulsory. If we waited long enough we would find the car rolling down the other side of the hump. This phenomenon is called [quantum] tunneling.[14]

It appears quantum effects have no small influence over the macro world in which we live. But there's a more fundamental problem ignored by Sapolsky in his claims about micro-macro state relations: science isn't sure about *precisely what physical laws* govern the micro-level of reality:

When we talk about the dynamical equations of motion we can talk about the specific example of the Newtonian dynamical equations of motion, we know *those are false. We could also talk about the non-relativistic quantum mechanical dynamical equations of motion, we know those are false. We could talk about the relativistic field theoretic dynamical equations of motion, we're pretty sure because of gravitation and because of problems with renormalization that those are false. So <u>we don't know yet what the true dynamic microscopic dynamical equations of motion are</u>. That... remains to be filled in.*[15] [emphasis added]

Sapolsky's claim that quantum effects can't "bubble up" to support macro-level indeterminism, and thus break the causal chain in support of free will, lacks scientific validation.

Part Three: Strong Emergence

Determinism is a reductive theory. How a system behaves is reducible to the activity of its constituent parts. Consciousness is thereby reducible to the play of elementary particles between our ears. Our thoughts reflect neural brain activity. There are other, non-reductive ways to view reality.

Strong emergence theory inverts micro-macro relations and turns the reductive paradigm on its head.[16] Higher level structures don't merely reflect the sum of their parts, but stand on their own. Their emergence brings forth *novelty* — properties, behavior, and principles which aren't reducible to the activity of their constituent parts. In the emergence paradigm, consciousness can't be reduced to neural brain activity.

In reductive theories, influence runs from the "bottom up" – lower-level constituents cause how higher-level systems behave. In the emergence paradigm, influence runs in both directions, both "bottom up" and "top down":

> *Top-down causation is the ability of higher levels of reality to have causal power over lower levels. An example is aircraft design: plans for a jumbo jet aircraft result in billions of atoms being deployed to create the aircraft. Thus abstract plans and entities, such as social agreements, are causally effective.*
>
> *Physically, money is just coins or pieces of paper with patterned marks on them. This does not explain its causal significance....which can cause physical change in the world such as the construction of buildings... based on social agreements that lead to the value of money. Meaning and purpose are abstract entities that form the highest level in the hierarchy of causation in the mind and in organizations.*[17]

The emergence paradigm thus challenges determinism's "bottom up" presumptions. Physical events can't explain the emergence of meaning, language, mathematics, and other "abstract entities".

> *The key feature of higher level of causation... is its use of language (spoken or written) and abstract symbolism. These are all irreducible higher-level variables... Intentional action then enables one to implement the resulting plans, and so change the physical world. Indeed, you could not be reading this chapter if it were not true: the marks on the paper that constitute the letters you are reading have the form they do because of top-down action from the mind to my hand. Wars will or will not be waged depending on ethical stances...so the nature of ethical stances has crucial effects in the way human activity impacts...the world.*

In terms of micro-macro level relations:

> *The role of that the microscopic laws play is a positive one, providing the order that allows the emergence of complex systems and delimiting the profile of possibilities of behavior that attach to those systems. When it comes to describing human capabilities, this way of thinking of the laws largely reinforces our pre-theoretic sense of what we can do.*[18]

Sapolsky rejects emergence theory by offering a *physical* model of emergence described in purely *physical* terms. His examples are primarily drawn from geometric, inanimate, and non-cognitive biological processes: slime molds expand, ant colonies procure food, manipulating geometric shapes (lines, triangles, etc.) in certain patterns create new shapes not contained therein, etc. A mechanical portrait of emergent phenomena is painted on a canvass of inanimate and non-cognitive processes.

When human behavior is involved, the mechanistic vocabulary breaks down. His city planning example involves laying out streets, schools, malls, parks, etc. Such activities necessarily engage *intentions, purposes, values,* and *judgements*. His descriptions avoid such non-physical factors by ignoring them: after all the planning is said and done, all we end up with is "a bunch of neurons in a mall clumped together".

Describing people as "clumps of neurons" begs the question – whether human behavior *is* reducible to "clumps of neurons" which dictate behavior. Insisting we're "neural clumps" is a circular description which precludes volitional factors, such as intentions and purposes, from entering the picture. How can the fact that factories weren't placed next to schools be explained without them? Because that's what some leptons wanted?

Sapolsky's example isn't evidence against free will – it merely describes behavior is mechanical terms in accordance with determinist premises.

Sapolsky sums up his objections to strong emergence theory in two neural clumps. [19]

- *First,* he argues that one "start state" produces only "one outcome". This presumes a non-probabilistic interpretation of quantum theory which, as discussed, is an open question subject to contention; and ignores the issues raised in this chapter regarding the limits of scientific knowledge concerning the natural order and scientific problems with the cosmic domino theory.

- *Second,* he objects that emergent systems can't simply "choose to do whatever they want". Bricks can't "stop being brick-ish". (P. 193 – 202) He's right, they can't; but no emergentist would claim otherwise. Higher-level structures needn't "do what they want" to bring forth novel properties and principles. Being constrained by lower-level constituents doesn't preclude transcending them. Bricks *must* remain "brick-ish" to provide the structural underpinning for emergent systems. They aren't *just* bricks in the wall....

Sapolsky is right, however, to complain that emergent theories are often, if not routinely, vague as to the mechanics of the emergent process. That he often "can't understand what they're suggesting" is a fair objection given such vagueness – especially regarding the process by which consciousness may have emerged from the physical realm. Emergentists often seem to be placing a conceptual overlay on the facts (as, notably, do determinists) that isn't in any apparent way derived from them.

On the other hand, Sapolsky's circular descriptions of non-cognitive processes aren't arguments against the emergence of self-conscious awareness. Nor do they help explain the existence of non-physical principles such as meaning, purpose, syntax, logic, and values – and why, most importantly, elementary particles in subatomic reality appear to be organizing themselves around and by way of such conceptual rules and abstract non-physical frameworks.

A tennis serve can be described in terms of physical bodily movements. But the description can't explain why the body is making those movements in service of playing tennis. This is where emergentist descriptions offer needed explanations for behavior that aren't available under determinist doctrine, by which all human behavior, regardless of type, is equally attributable to impersonal causal forces.

> *Top-down causation is ubiquitous in physics, chemistry, and biology, because the outcome of lower-level interactions is always determined by context.*[20]

Strong emergence offers a credible, if rudimentary and less than satisfactory, scientific framework by which human volition could be situated in the physical world. Its further development should be expected to offer a credible challenge to determinist doctrine and its inability to explain human behavior in terms of motivation, purposes, and reason.

Part Four: Causal Circularity

The *choice violates physics* argument is often presented with a ferociousness that serves to mask its inherent circularity.

> *We do not guess, <u>we know</u> that brains are made of particles. We do not guess, <u>we know</u> that we can derive from the laws for the constituents what the whole object does. If you make a claim to the contrary, you are contradicting well-established science (underscoring added).*[21]

This sounds like an argument, but isn't.

It's a determinist declaration that consists of three claims, each of which presumes determinism true:

- *"Brains are made of particles"*

True, but this goes without saying. No free will advocate would argue otherwise. That's what brains *are*. The question is whether consciousness is something *more than* mere brain particles. Assuming that our mental lives can be reduced to the play of elementary brain particles begs the question.

- *"Objects [obey] the laws [of their] constituents"*

True, if we're talking about physical events. The question is whether consciousness is nothing more than how its physical constituents behave. Assuming that's the case begs the question.

- *"[Free will] is contradicting well-established science"*

Not true, except under a selective interpretation of science – an interpretation subject to heated contention and about which there is no consensus. The claim is belied by the more than two dozen quantum theories scrapping over whether the universe is deterministic, precluding human intervention, or probabilistic, and thus admitting of the possibility.

If free will were known to violate science, one must question why so many prominent physicists refuse to endorse determinism or rule out the capacity for choice.

Are those physicists *contradicting science?*

If so, should those amongst them who've won Nobel prizes consider giving them back?...

Part Five: Undermining Science

There's plenty of evidence that free will exists. The question is what kind of evidence should be considered meaningful.

Conventional wisdom endorses a questionable dichotomy: if there's credible evidence for a physical event, it's provisionally presumed to exist pending further investigation. Evidence derived from experience is another matter – it's presumed suspect, unreliable, and often casually tossed away without further ado.

This overlooks the fact that science is a *human endeavor* that takes place *in consciousness*. It stems from *experiential reports* made by consciousness. Observation, verification, and theorizing are consequent to *conscious experience* and *human convention*, including language, principles of reason, and conceptual frameworks.

The appearance of causal patterns requires human *intervention*. Causal pathways arise from holding one set of variables constant, which intervention fixes the initial point of departure for measurement:

> *Causal information tells us how the state of a system would be affected by interventions...Causal structure tells us how manipulating the value of one variable induces changes in others. The possibility of causal knowledge rests on the fact that we can effectively isolate systems in the laboratory, manipulate... external input...and observe the effects...Global laws tell us how the system as a whole evolves if not interfered with, whereas causal knowledge tells us what happens when it is interfered with.*[22]

That doesn't make science subjective. It means that it requires human intervention and is predicated upon a series of reasoned judgements made by conscious subjects. Data means nothing without the assignment of *meaning* and *significance*.[23]

Scientific inquiry is equally driven by human values – the yearning for knowledge and the valuing of reason, investigation, evidence, objectivity, accuracy, methodology, verification, etc.

From Irwin Schrodinger, one of the founding fathers of quantum mechanics:

> *There is a tendency to forget that all science is bound up with human culture in general and that scientific findings, even...the most advanced and esoteric and difficult to grasp, are meaningless outside their cultural context.*[24]

Science requires a thinking subject capable of assuming an objective viewpoint. That *isn't possible* in a determined universe because we can't control our thoughts, and our judgements consist of compelled beliefs forced upon us by predetermined physical events. We discover what we're caused to believe we've discovered.

In a world of compelled thoughts, scientific theories don't predict how reality behaves – they reflect what we're caused to believe about how it behaves.

If determinism is true, *science isn't possible.*

Rocks can't study rocks. [25]

Part Six: The Limits of Science

How Does Water Freeze?

Come on...don't tell me scientists don't know that!

Yes – surprising as it may be, physics is uncertain about why hot water freezes faster than cold. But how *could* hot water get there faster? Isn't cold water already half the way there?

Physics doesn't have clue:

Who would have thought there's still any question about the freezing of water, you know? So those of you who think that physics is done, we're not even done with understanding how water freezes, so there's a long way to go.[26]

Once scientists figure out the basics about water, we might ask them if, per chance, they've been able to figure anything out about free will....

Part Seven: Conclusion

Ever been to a fortune teller?

(Since you're reading this and most likely alone, you need only admit it to yourself....)

So, imagine a fortune teller at the turn of the last century. A physicist approaches and offers up the required coin. The teller is asked to forecast what the state of physics will be in another 100 years.

The physicist hears the forecast – that moving clocks run slow, that moving objects shrink, that space-time is curved, that matter behaves like waves and particle, that 95% of the visible universe can't be seen, that empty space has energy values, that particles can jump through impenetrable barriers and can instantly influence each other without physical contact while galaxies apart.

What would the physicist do?

First, demand all the money back.

Second, go the nearest speakeasy and get entangled with several rounds of whiskey.

And *third*, conclude that the forecast was even less likely than leprechauns or fairy dust….

Chapter Seven

THE CONTRADICTORY NATURE OF DETERMINIST CLAIMS

THE HEADLINES

Determinist claims are self-contradictory. They belong to a class of self-defeating claims that affirm two contradictory principles at once. Determinists claim *determinism is true,* but also claim *our beliefs about what's true are caused by forces beyond our control.* Thus, by their own terms, they are causally compelled to believe in determinism. They are determinists because it was predestined - not because it's true. By reducing thoughts to unthinking physical events, determinism undermines the basis for all truth claims - including its own. There's no way to know what's true in a world where all beliefs are the product of physical events which don't think, don't reason, or have any conception about the meaning of truth.

Part One: The Fundamental Flaw

There's a fundamental flaw in determinism. It's a fatal one, and for which there's no resolution –

Determinist principles are self-contradictory.

Due to self-application, they drain themselves of any truth value. The mechanics of self-invalidation work as follows:

By determinist doctrine, our thoughts are causal effects generated by physical forces. Our mental lives are "given to us by the cosmos": we think what we're *caused to* think, believe what we're *caused to* believe. What we experience arises from neural activity in our brain – physical events caused by prior physical events in a chain that originated at the Big Bang.

This includes *all* our beliefs – including our *beliefs about what's true*. We believe true whatever we're caused to believe true. Our thoughts about what's true are produced by physical forces and we can't believe otherwise. By determinism doctrine, we believe what we're told.

This includes determinist claims. They have no special exemption. The belief *"determinism is true"* is no less a byproduct of unthinking causal forces than any other thought.

Hence the self-contradiction at the heart of every determinist claim and principle:

No determinist could ever know whether determinism is true: by their own terms, they are compelled to believe determinism true and can't believe otherwise.

By determinist principles, those who believe in determinism do so because *they must*, not because *it's true*. No belief is privileged in a universe where thoughts are beyond anyone's control.

What we think has merit in causal reality is whatever we're caused to believe meritorious. Reason, explanation, justification, and judgement are without value: they are causally compelled beliefs about other causally compelled beliefs – our conviction in their merit is no less the product of physical forces than the causally compelled beliefs they presume to validate.

Determinists are thus trapped by their own net, which knows no bounds. By determinist precepts, determinists are:

- *Forced to believe in determinism.*

- *Forced to believe that free will is nonsense.*

- *Forced to believe their position conceptually sound and backed by compelling science.*

- *Forced to believe that free will advocates are, shall we say, woefully misguided.*

Determinists therefore reject the notion of free will not because it doesn't exist, or because its existence would violate the cosmic order: they reject it because they *can't believe otherwise*. If our thoughts and actions are determined, there is no other reason why anyone could believe anything true.

The insurmountable challenge for those who proselytize for the causal faith can be stated as follows:

How can anyone know if human behavior is determined if they're causally compelled to believe it is (or isn't)?

If you stumble across a determinist who insists they can answer the question, ask them the following after whatever answer they venture to give:

That's an interesting thought. Why do you believe it true? By determinist doctrine, our thoughts are compelled by causal forces, in which case you were caused to believe it true. Indeed, you can't believe otherwise - regardless of what the truth might be. There's no point in discussing it further if you're incapable of stating anything that's based on truth - not on what you've been caused to believe true by predetermined events beyond your control. By your own doctrine, nothing you say is credible.

If they persist that you've got it wrong and seek to justify their answer, repeat the above response. If they respond yet again, follow same instructions.
Keep repeating as necessary....

―――――――

Self-defeating claims trip over themselves.

They tie themselves in a knot because, by their own terms, they apply to *themselves,* and to *the person* making them.[1]

Consider the determinist claim:

"Our thoughts are caused by forces beyond our control."

If that's the case, then it's no less true of *that very thought itself*. Hence the contradiction behind the claim:

I'm causally compelled to believe that our beliefs are causally compelled.

The rug is thus pulled out from under all truth claims. Determinism leaves us without any objective, *rational basis* to believe anything true – whether it be determinist claims or otherwise. The foundation for all rational precepts on which we rely in living our lives is undermined:

- *What is rational? Whatever we're caused to believe has a rational basis.*

- *What are facts? Whatever we're caused to believe factual.*

- *What is evidence? Whatever we're caused to believe of evidentiary value.*

- *What is objective? Whatever we're caused to believe doesn't depend on us.*

- *What is valuable? Whatever we're caused to believe has value.*

- *What is reality? Whatever we're caused to believe real.*

The self-defeating nature of determinist claims isn't part of popular discussions on the topic. Harris and Sapolsky don't mention or address the problem. They boldly declare we don't control our thoughts, or that they're the product of biology and environment – forgetting that this would apply to *those claims*, in which they are equally forced to believe

It seems they were predestined to ignore the matter.

The self-contradictory nature of determinist claims is based on two conflicting assertions:

- ***I know that determinism is true.***

- ***What I believe true is whatever I've been caused to believe true.***

What does this mean for the free will debate?

By determinist doctrine, it's simply a conflict *among causally compelled beliefs*. It's a contest in which the parties champion whatever beliefs they've been caused to believe and reject those which they're caused to believe nonsensical or foolhardy.

The debate isn't about resolving the truth. It's not about convincing anyone of anything. It's not about cogent reasoning or principled judgements. It's nothing more than the predestined mechanical unspooling of thoughts and actions put into play at the Big Bang.

Sapolsky was recently confronted about the problem, noted in an opening statement of debate along with numerous other objections to determinist doctrine. In responding to the list of challenges, Sapolsky didn't address the matter. He greeted with silence the most fundamental of conceptual challenges to determinist claims.[2] The omission is no less glaring in the five hundred plus pages of *Determined*.

The issue is equally neglected by free will advocates, who are no less complicit in the silence.[3]

Part Two: Conventional Wisdoms

Self-contradictory claims are everywhere.

You don't have to look very far. They routinely masquerade as conventional wisdoms. They are repeated so often that we unconditionally endorse them without realizing that they are self-contradictory, and make no sense.

Some well-worn examples:

- *"You can't trust anyone."*

If so, then you can't trust the speaker either.

The next time you hear someone say this, you might consider responding:

Alright – but then I can't trust you or your claim. Thanks for warning me that you're untrustworthy....

- *"Nobody knows anything."*

If so, then the speaker can't know anything either.

The next time you hear someone say this, you might consider responding:

Okay – but then you can't know that, either. You have no idea if your claim is true. Go waste someone else's time ...

- *"There are no truths."*

If so, then this claim *can't be true* either.

The next time you hear someone say this, you might consider responding:

Okay – then what you just said can't be true, either. Why you're admitting your claim isn't true is beyond me, but go peddle your wares elsewhere...

Part Three: Cultural and Political Contradictions

Performative contradictions can be found behind most social, cultural, political, and spiritual movements.

Here's a few tried and true classics:

- **"Beliefs reflect class bias." (Marxism)**

If so, then that belief merely reflects the class bias of Marxist advocacy.

The next time a Marxist says this – unless it's a Marx Brother – you might consider responding:

Okay – then that claim reflects your class bias. It's no more truthful than any other class belief. Hypocrites of the world, unite!

- **"All is interpretation." (Deconstructionism)**

If so, then this is just another relativist interpretation, no more reflective of truth than any other.

The next time a deconstructionist accosts you at Starbucks, you might consider responding:

Alright – then that's simply your interpretation. If that's all, it's no more justified than anyone else's. Like something else I can think of, everybody has one...

- *"Truth is a means of gaining power and control." (Post-modernism)*

If so, then the speaker is attempting to overpower and control you by insisting it's true. The next time someone tries to dominate you with this one, you might consider responding:

I see... so then you're telling me this in order to gain power and control over me. Thanks for the warning, I'll conduct myself accordingly!

Part Four: Determinist Contradictions

Determinist claims are no less contradictory.

They are garden variety performative contradictions, nothing special.

Some examples, expressed as Harris and Sapolsky frame them:

- *Our thoughts are not of our making.* (p. 37)

In that case, *that very thought* isn't of the determinist's making. It emerged from unknown background conditions, not from knowledge of what's true.

The determinist is asserting a self-invalidating performative contradiction,

My belief that our thoughts aren't of our making is not of my making.

- *You are not in control of your mind.* (p. 5)

In that case, determinists asserting this claim are conceding they're not in control of *their minds* when making the claim. This isn't the best testimonial…if they don't control their minds, how could they know the claim's true?

Any answer to this would come from a mind they concede isn't under their control….

Determinists are asserting the self-invalidating performative contradiction,

I'm not in control of my mind right in my telling you that we're not in control of our minds.

- *Unconscious neural events determine our thoughts and actions.* (p. 16)

In that case, unconscious neural activity are causing determinists to make this claim. By the claim's terms, it was dictated by neural events and not based on what's true.

The determinist is asserting a self-invalidating performative contradiction,

Unconscious neural events are causing me to believe that my thoughts are caused by unconscious neural events.

- *Some moments before you are aware of what you will do next...your brain has already determined what you will do.* (pp. 7-9)

In that case, whenever determinists praise the causal faith or declare free will illusory, it's because moments before their brains dictated they'd do so.

Their conviction is based on causal coercion from the gray matter between their ears – not inquiry, investigation, reason, or knowledge.

The determinist claim about brain bullying is the self-invalidating performative contradiction,

Moments ago my brain determined that I'd be claiming right now that our brains determine what we'll do next.

TIME OUT FOR A MOMENT OF LEGALITIES:

Under determinist principles, I *didn't write* this book.

It was written by *my brain*, which determined each sentence I'd write just moments before my fingers hit the keys. This is of great concern to me, though my brain already knows that.

Here's what I'm wondering about:

- If my brain wrote this book moments before I put it down, can it sue me for copyright infringement?

- If it does, won't my brain also have to defend the claim?

- If so, doesn't my brain have a conflict of interest?

- Is it any defense that my brain knew what I was about to do and didn't stop me?

- Who pays the lawyer? And do they have to get paid twice?

END OF TIME OUT

- *My mental life is simply given to me by the cosmos.* (p. 19)

In that case, the cosmos gifted to determinists the belief this claim is true. Their convictions aren't based on investigation or knowledge – but upon a cosmic gift they have no choice but to believe true.

As in *The Godfather*, it's a gift that can't be refused.

The determinist performative contradiction being asserted is,

My belief that my mental life was given to me by the cosmos was given to me by the cosmos.

- *To be convinced by an argument is to be subjugated by it.* (Making Sense Podcast, #241)

In that case, Harris is subjugated by *that argument*. He believes it because it was predestined he'd believe it – not because it's true. The self-invalidating performative contradiction is,

I am subjugated by the argument that "we're subjugated by the arguments we believe in".

According to Harris, merit has nothing to do with why we believe in arguments. It's a matter of *causal dominion*.

Determinist have no special exemption, or at least none on record. If we're all subjugated by the arguments we believe in, so are determinists. The cosmos doesn't play favorites.

Are you subjugated by this argument?

Or have you been subjugated by an argument to the contrary?

Part Five: Don't Forget the Speaker

Self-defeating claims get in trouble because they forget they apply to themselves. That's what creates the contradiction, but it's not always obvious. We hear them so often about so many different matters that we accept them in the ordinary course.

But make the self-application explicit and their contradictory nature jumps off the page. Spelling it out doesn't change the meaning – it states what they really *do mean*. The self-contradiction is glaring when stated expressly:

- "My belief that our thoughts originate outside consciousness originated outside my consciousness."

- "Physical events give rise to my conviction that physical events give rise to our convictions."

- "I'm not the author of my belief that we are not the authors of our beliefs."

- "My belief that our thoughts are caused by neural events we don't control was caused by neural events I don't control."

- "We watch our thoughts arise as if from the void, which is a thought I'm watching as if arising from the void."

- "People assume an illusory authorship of their thoughts, which I'm assuming about this thought."

- "There are truths appropriate to every occasion, which is a truth appropriate to this occasion."

- *"I can't act otherwise than insisting that I can't act otherwise."*

- *""The future was set at the Big Bang, including my statement that the future was set at the Big Bang."*

- *"Explanations are after-the-fact stories, including this explanation, which is an after-the-fact story."*

- *"Truth is what we're caused to believe true, which is what I've been caused to believe true."*

- *"My belief that we're nothing other than our cumulative biological and environmental luck, is a product of my cumulative biological and environmental luck."*

In similar fashion, every determinist principle invalidates the truth of what it's asserting.

Question for your neighborhood determinist:

You're a determinist, is it? Tell me, are you prepared to admit you've been caused to believe in determinism by prior conditions beyond your control and that you can't believe otherwise?

If they're not prepared to admit it, tell them they're not a determinist: they're rejecting its central principle.

If they admit their thoughts are beyond their control, ask them how they know....

Part Six: Alien Control

Did you know we're *controlled by aliens*?

It's true. They control every thought we have. Yes – they beam them into our heads from anti-gravity thought-projection devices in 12th dimensional space-time. You haven't heard? I bet you think I'm kidding. I'm not.

And a large body of evidence says I'm right: Lights in the sky. Tales of abduction. Crop circles. Fast food salads....

Still don't believe it? If you're a determinist, you'd best think twice before saying no: the belief in determinism *is no more credible than claims of alien dominion*. Not a gamma ray more credible.

Both claims are self-contradictory. Both equally place control over our thoughts in outside hands. Both equally disqualify us from knowing whether they're true. The logical contradiction is the same:

- *I don't control my beliefs and what I think true is in outside hands.*

- *But I know it's true that X [fill in the blank] is causing me to believe this.*

There's a problem here. If we don't control our thoughts, how could we know who or what's controlling them?

If you think it *more likely* we're controlled by biology and environment than, say, by hairless creatures from Mars, you're in a bind – you're conceding you don't control your thoughts, in which case you can't know what's controlling us, be it Martians or otherwise. Once you place your thoughts in outside hands, what *you think* is controlling you is whatever you're *caused to believe.*

So maybe it's Martians. Maybe not. Perhaps it was Zeus all along. Or Voldemort. Maybe it's the Wizard of Oz, making you believe it's the man behind the curtain….

Why would anyone in that position ever identify themselves, rather than put the blame elsewhere? It doesn't figure to reason.

If *you* were controlling human affairs, given the state of the world today…wouldn't *you* opt for *plausible deniability*?

Part Seven: Are We Really *Biochemical Robots*?

Harris maintains we are mechanical devices comprised of living tissue – mere *biochemical robots*.

The claim is a run of the mill performative contradiction: by determinist terms, *what* we believe about human nature is whatever we're *caused to* believe.

This is the rabbit hole of determinism.

All claims about who or what we are instantly disqualify themselves from being true:

- *It's true, we are biochemical robots.*

- *I believe that's what we are because I was pre-programmed to believe it.*

The only thing a determinist can say consistent with determinist doctrine is,

We are not biochemical robots. We have no idea what we are and can't ever know - our thoughts are forced upon us by physical events and what we believe we are is whatever we're caused to think we are at any given moment. But don't take my word for it, check back with me in an hour. I might have been predestined to believe I'm something or somebody altogether different by then....

If our beliefs are in the hands of forces beyond our control, we can't know *who or what we are.*

That's my belief, but I may be saying this without any idea about who or what I am...

The Perfect Prediction Machine

Determinism is a faith-based gospel.

Its adherents bow to the gods of causal subjugation.

As Harris concedes, they've been *subjugated* by the argument that we live in a clockwork universe and that free will is a naïve and ill-gained illusion.

Harris imagines a way to prove determinism true. *Free Will* conceives of a "perfect neuro-imaging device" that would predict our thoughts and behavior in advance:

> *[Such a machine] would allow us to detect and interpret the subtlest changes in brain function...[and] produce a complete record of what you would think and do some moments in advance of each event...demonstrating that the experimenter knew what you would think and do just before you did. (p. 11)*

Wouldn't these findings offer rock solid proof we're *biochemical robots?*

In fact, it wouldn't prove a thing. The hypothetical is a *dramatized self-contradiction*. The findings indicate our thoughts are generated by external forces beyond our control – in which case, whether or not we believe the findings is equally out of our hands.

The performative contradiction is,

> *I believe in the machine's findings not because of reasoning or judgement, but because I'm caused to believe in them by prior neural activity. If that neural activity should change, but the circumstances surrounding the findings remain the same, I would believe otherwise.*

All bets are off in a causal universe. You can't *know* what's true if you're caused to believe what you think true.

If you don't believe me, ask the aliens....

.

Personal Identity

A determined universe is a Causal Matrix.

There's no limit to what we can be made to believe. Is the world real? Does anyone else exist? Do we have a past? Is it the same past we had yesterday?

Personal identity is no less illusory.

Are we the same person we were last week? Or five minutes ago? Are we going to be the same person tomorrow? Does everyone randomly exchange identities every other Tuesday? Thursdays? What about leap years?

The ultimate determinist irony:

Any determinist who thinks they *know who they are* doesn't *believe* in determinism.

I Think, Therefore Who Knows?

What about the famous *I Think Therefore I Am*?

It's no different than any other belief. Determinism reduces the most celebrated claim in Western philosophy to a causally compelled belief devoid of merit.

The *I Think* claim is even *less reliable* than most. It rests on many causally compelled assumptions:

Selves exist. Thoughts exist. Reason exists. Truth exists. Existence exists. We can know what's true. The I Think is True. I can't be fooled I'm thinking these thoughts. Etc.

It rests on just as many causally compelled dualisms that we're forced into believing true:

Consciousness – World. Reality – Illusion. Self – No-self. Doing – Being. Thinking – Observing. Connected – Unrelated. Order – Chaos. Stasis – Change. Etc.

Determinists can't declare the *I think* true without repudiating determinism, which attributes truth solely to what causal forces dictate. Come to think of it, they can't declare that the *I think* isn't true, either....

The only thing a determinists can say is,

I think, therefore I'm subjugated.

Part Eight: The Wasteland

Many theories besides determinism are laid to predestined dust by self-defeating contradictions. In addition to those mentioned above, these include:

- *Physicalism* – If everything is physical, then that statement is a non-physical, conceptual claim that has no meaning.

- *Empiricism* – If all knowledge comes from sensory experience, then this claim isn't based on knowledge because it's conceptual and not derived from sensory experience.

- *Pragmatism* – By its terms, we should only believe in pragmatism if it's pragmatic to do so, not because it's true.

- *Skepticism* – If skepticism is the proper approach in life, then we must be skeptical about whether it's the proper approach.

- *Logical Positivism* – If claims are meaningless unless objectively verifiable, then this claim is meaningless because it can't be objectively verified.

- *The Matrix* – If we believe we're living in an illusory world, then we can't trust the evidence leading to that conclusion, which would equally be illusory.

In defense of determinists, it may be said they have a better excuse for championing self-invalidating claims than these other belief systems:

They can't do otherwise.

Is the Use of Reason Reasonable?

Finally, there's the matter of *reason* itself.

Seeking to discredit the value of reason is contradictory and self-defeating – *one would have to use reason to discredit it.*

This puts to pasture all claims that seek to reduce reason and rational discourse to subjective, relative, psychological, or arbitrary points of view.

> *It is usually a good strategy to ask whether a general claim about truth or meaning applies to itself. We cannot criticize…claims of reason without employing reason at some other point to formulate and support such criticisms.*[4]

It's my subjective opinion this is reasonable.

Part Nine: Conclusion

Determinism is based on a logical error:

We can't reduce ourselves to physical events without the use of reason, meaning, and significance –*non-physical* byproducts reflecting physical processes without independent influence.

Hence the absurdity of the determinist project:

The attempt to use *non-physical* rules of syntax to convey non-physical meanings in order to influence *non-physical* thoughts appealing to *non-physical* reasons.

Determinists mean to say that meaning doesn't have meaning. It's a physical byproduct of physical events following the laws of physics without regard to conceptual principles. The determinist project is thus fundamentally absurd.

What do determinists say to all this?

They don't. It's off the radar in popular discourse, for determinists and free will advocates alike.

Postmodernist schools of thought, by contrast, are routinely criticized for their self-contradictory claims. They maintain that truth doesn't exist; that it's a means to power, a device employed to manipulate others and gain control over them. The self-contradiction at the heart of the postmodernist movement has been widely noted: claiming "truth doesn't exist" is affirming a truth, which isn't possible if it doesn't exist.

Yet the charge is virtually never leveled against determinism, which suffers from the same logical error and is no less contradictory.

Noam Chomsky makes a rare invocation of the performative contradiction in illustrating the absurdity of determinist thinking:

> *There's a lot of arguments that we don't have freedom of the will. The literature is kind of interesting for the reasons William James discussed: If you really believe there's no freedom of the will, why bother to present an argument? You're just forced to do it, and the person you're talking to can't be convinced because there's no such thing as reasons. So why not watch a ballgame.[5]*

Anyone for a Dodger dog?

POP KOANS

In lieu of a Pop Quiz, it seems fitting to close a chapter on contradictions with some newly minted Zen koans inspired by determinist thinking:

Do you need to control your mind to claim you don't control it?

If you don't control your mind, what mind are you using when you claim you're not controlling it?

How do you know you're a determinist if you're caused to believe you are?

Could you be caused to believe something that you really don't believe?

Could it be true that we don't know what's true?

What is a choice that "comes out of darkness" choosing?

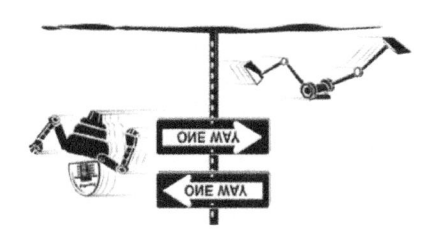

Chapter Eight

HAVING IT BOTH WAYS

THE HEADLINES

Harris and Sapolsky make numerous suggestions which violate determinist doctrine and presuppose free will. Their prescriptions make no sense if we lack the capacity for reason and choice. They insist that we can *change our lives, plan for the future, rectify problems, protect the innocent, punish wrongdoing, even face the fact we don't have free will.* Such claims employ free will terms that have no relevance in predestined reality and presuppose that we can form intentions, direct our behavior, and aim at achieving the goals we value. Using free will terms may make determinism appear more palatable, but jumping back and forth between a determined world and one in which we have the capacity for choice is having it both ways.

Part One: Try Acting Like a Determinist!

No one is a determinist. Nobody!

Those who say they are, aren't. Those who say they aren't – well, they aren't either…

When they're not theorizing about causal chains, determinists are just like everyone else. They wake up, exercise, shower, dress, work, return home, dine – and perhaps most important, decide if it's going to be a Netflix or Showtime evening.

They spend every moment living their lives on the basis that they have free will.

They're only determinists *in their heads*.

Nothing else is possible. A simple experiment easily proves this:

Try acting like you are determined. Stop deciding anything. Stop judging anything. Stop directing your thoughts or experiences and pretend they are being controlled by an outside source. Set an alarm and see if you can make it for 15 minutes.

Here's the rules:

No decisions means *no decisions*.

No wondering about when the time is up – if you do, you'd have to decide whether to keep going or not.

And no cheating by meditating – who do you think would be bringing your attention back to your breath or mantra when it wanders off for a frolic?

Give it a try. Not deciding isn't as easy as you might think. Determinists can't do it either. They are determinists *in name only*. By their actions, they reveal themselves to be the most ardent of free will advocates. They live their lives based on *the conviction* they have free will and, as with others, *can influence* the course of affairs.

Perhaps they were predestined to be in denial....

Part Two: *Free Will-Speak*

Nobody wants to be a *biochemical robot*.

It means being enslaved by causal dominion. It means having no say in your thoughts or actions. It means being blamed for any number of things you do – even though you didn't choose to do it and couldn't do otherwise.

There's nothing fun or sexy about perpetual victimhood. How do you package disempowerment to make it attractive? How do determinists inspire new disciples to enthusiastically embrace complete causal servitude?

It's the usual solution – good P.R.

Determinists thus invented a new language to help sell causal servitude: *free will-speak.*

It borrows words from the free will paradigm and uses them to describe causal events. It waives a causal wand over the world and, presto, allows determinists to boldly declare we can *choose, plan, create, demand, change, rectify, encourage, punish, discard thoughts, adopt truths, etc.*

How is any of this possible if we don't control what we think, intend, or do? That's where the magic of *free will-speak* comes in. It uses free will terms to evoke an aura of free will activities, and everyone feels good about living in a mechanical universe where nobody can influence anything. *Free will-speak* transforms a cold, mechanical wasteland into a magical land of hope, fantasy, and opportunity. It puts a happy face on causal dominion.

Perpetual victimhood sounds even better than Disneyworld!

This *is* effective marketing....

Part Three: Free Will-Speak Claims

The following claims in *Free Will* and *Determined* display the art of *free will-speak* at its finest:

- ***You can change your life, and yourself, through effort and discipline.*** *(p. 38)*

Suddenly we have the ability to take deliberate action and marshal the forces of effort and discipline. What happened to the inability to control our actions? How can change things in a world where everything's been predestined and nothing can change?

The only thing a determinist can say consistent with determinist doctrine is,

We can be causally compelled to have the illusory experience of changing our lives with effort and discipline, but our thoughts and actions are determined and we can't change anything.

The only thing *needing* change is the idea *we can* change anything in causal reality…

- *The freedom to do what one intends…is no less valuable than it ever was. (p. 13)*

Suddenly we can form intentions and freely take action to implement them. Where did that ability come from? How is that possible if our behavior is the causal product of biology mixed with environment?

The only thing a determinist can say consistent with determinist doctrine is,

We can be causally compelled to believe we have valuable freedoms and can follow our intentions, but these are illusory

experiences caused by predestined physical forces.

What *would be* valuable is to disregard all claims about "valuable freedoms" in a world where no freedoms exist.

- *We need to accept the absurdity of hating anyone for anything they've done. (Sapolsky, p. 402)*

What happened to the idea that our thoughts are in the hands of causal forces beyond our control? If that's really the case, we wouldn't be capable of evaluating and determining what's absurd and what isn't.

The only thing a determinist can say consistent with determinist doctrine is,

What we believe absurd is whatever we're caused to believe the case, and if we hate people for what they've done it's because we've been predestined to believe it justified.

The only thing we need to accept as absurd is the idea we can judge something absurd if we don't control what we think about anything.

- *Having a gun to your head is still a problem worth rectifying, wherever intentions come from.* (Harris, p. 13)

Even Ray Donovan can't rectify anything in a causal universe. Now we have the ability to identify problems, consider solutions, and take remedial action? In a world that's predestined and can't be influenced?

If the *free will-speak* were dropped out of respect for ideological consistency, the claim would have to be reframed as follows:

> **We can be causally compelled to believe a gun to our head is a problem to rectify, but we only think it a "problem" because we've been caused to believe it – nothing can be rectified in a causal universe where everything's predestined.**

The only thing in need of rectification is the idea that we *can rectify* anything in causal reality...

- *The approach that makes the most sense to me is the idea of quarantine. The public needs to be protected...justifying the constraint on... freedom, [which should be] done in a way that constraints the least.* (Sapolsky, p. 349)

It seems we have a determinist, whose thoughts are caused by neural activity, making moral assertions about "protecting the public" and "constraining freedom the least" when so doing. How is "protecting" anything possible if everything is predestined? What "freedom" is there to constrain in the first place if free will doesn't exist and our thoughts and behavior causally compelled?

Drop the *free will-speak* and reframe the claim true to determinist doctrine, and you have:

Biology and environment can cause us to believe that protecting people is worthwhile and what's the best way to go about it. In truth, nobody can be protected from harm because everything that befalls anyone has

already been predetermined and isn't susceptible to influenced.

What needs to be quarantined is claims that we protect people from harm in a predestined world where we can't protect anything.

- *We have shown that we can subtract out a belief that actions are freely, willfully, chosen, as we've become more knowledgeable, more reflecting, more modern.* (Sapolsky, p. 382)

Since when did we acquire the ability to direct our thoughts and add or subtract anything about the way we think? Weren't our thoughts supposed to be in the hands of causal forces beyond our control?

If the *free will-speak* were jettisoned, the only thing a determinist could say consistent with determinist doctrine is,

Causal forces can compel us to believe we are gaining knowledge, discarding naïve beliefs, and adopting a more modern approach - but these are illusory

experiences caused by predetermined forces beyond our control.

What *really* needs to be "subtracted" from the equation is claims that we can add or subtract from thoughts we don't have the ability to control.

- *You can create a framework in which certain decisions are more likely than others.* (Harris, p. 38)

Now we can direct our actions and arrange circumstances in a way that influences future events. How can we influence the likelihood of something that has either been predestined to happen or not? How can we make *present* decisions that affect *future* decisions if choice is illusory?
I think I need to sit down a moment...
Without the *free will-speak*, abiding by determinist doctrine would require the claim be reframed as follows:

Causal forces can compel us believe we are creating conditions that influence likelihoods, but nothing can change a predetermined future and "likelihoods" don't exist in a world where everything that happens is 100% certain to, and everything that doesn't was 100% certain not to.

In causal reality, there's simply *no likelihood* of our changing the likelihood of anything.

- **Clearly, we can respond intelligently to the threat posed by dangerous people without lying to ourselves about the ultimate origins of human behavior.** (Harris, p. 56)

Suddenly we can take anticipatory actions and respond to threats. How can we determine who's dangerous, and ward off potential harm, if all harms that will ever befall us have already been predestined to occur?

If determinists were to drop the *free-will speak*, they'd have to reframe the claim as follows for consistency with determinist doctrine:

Causal forces can compel us to believe we are responding intelligently to threats, but our responses are dictated by causal force and, in any case, can't do anything to prevent whatever harms were predestined to befall us.

I believe this is the *only* intelligent response to claims about responding intelligently in causal reality.

- *All of this needs to be reformed...and the people in the trenches trying to do it...are amazing.* (Sapolsky, p. 343)

Who's doing the reform? Who is making the suggestion? Who is making a moral stand based on current injustice? Who's controlling their actions to marshal the forces of reform "in the trenches"? Free will activities redolently abound. Thank god. How could reform otherwise occur?

Framing the claim consistent with determinist would yield a very different message:

We can be caused to believe reforms are needed, that we can effectuate them, a that amazing people are already doing so. But these are causally compelled beliefs, not objective statements about reality - and tomorrow we

> ***could be caused to adopt a diametrically opposed position.***

What needs reform is the idea that reform is possible in a clausal universe.

- *We can change…we have done this before, where we grew to recognize the true causes of something and, in the process, shed hate and blame and desire for retribution. (Sapolsky, p. 301)*

We can change? Who's the we? Why the active tense? If our behavior is determined, we *can't* change. We can only *suffer* change.

Sapolsky elsewhere subdues the rhetoric, conceding we can't change:

"We don't change our minds…our minds are changed by circumstances around us." (Sapolsky, p. 268).

Nevertheless, Chapter 12, the first of three chapters in *Determined* that concern change, begins as follows:

> *To get people to think differently about moral responsibility.... and the notion of our being free agents...to feel differently about those issues...and most of all, <u>to change fundamental aspects of how we behave.</u> (p. 268)*

So we *can't* change. Yet Sapolsky is *himself,* self-admittedly, attempting to influence others to "think differently" about determinism. How does someone "get people" to think differently other than by *taking action* (perhaps, even, to write a book about determinism?) in a universe where nobody can think otherwise?

In Chapter 13, Sapolsky recounts how the understanding epilepsy, schizophrenia, and autism changed history. It's an activist story in which people wanted change, gathered resources, conducted research, instituted social policies, and along the way *sedated* subjects....*decided* to become experts....*quit* medical establishments....*wrote* books....*donated* funds for....*constructed* mental health clinics.... Celebrities *came out* for the cause, and *we subtracted* blame from the equation.

So don't be discouraged. *We can* think differently *to change* how we behave. Remember – *we have done this before*!

It's amazing what clumps of amygdalas can do when they hang out together.

No free will advocate would argue that we can't be *changed by circumstances*. Nothing in chapters 12 – 14 does anything to assuage the principal fear posed by determinism – that we are powerless to do anything, whether changing ourselves or otherwise. To be consistent with determinist doctrine, Sapolsky's claim would require reframing:

The forces of biology and environment can cause us to think we're changing ourselves, growing, and learning to recognizing new truths - none of which is possible because our experiences are generated by predetermined causal forces beyond our control.

It's time to *recognize* a new truth: *we must change* the way we understand "we can change" whenever the phrase issues from the mouth of a determinist advocate.

- *A wide variety of human behaviors can be modified by punishments and incentives.* (Harris, p. 59)

Suddenly we can take deliberate action and use the proverbial carrot and stick to influence others? When did we gain control over our actions? How are we able to influence anything if everything's already been predetermined?

The only thing a determinist can say consistent with determinist doctrine is,

Causal events force us to believe we can influence others using the proverbial carrot and stick – but that's not possible because we don't control our actions and everyone's behavior was set at the Big Bang and beyond influence.

What we *could use* is punishments and incentives to stop determinists from making claims about influencing others in a causal universe....

- *I think it is essential that we face our lack of free will.* (Sapolsky, p. 391)

This is a curious claim: a determinist, who doesn't believe we have free will or can control our thoughts, is attempting to persuade us, by the use of reason, that we should *consider* the matter and *accept* that we don't have free will.

If we're free will advocates, we're being asked to *reconsider* our viewpoint and "face facts" – by someone who insists we have no such ability, that our thoughts are dictated by brain events, biology and environment.

Shorn of the *free will-speak*, Sapolsky would have to say:

Whatever we think we're facing, or refusing to face, is determined by biological and environmental forces beyond our control – no less so than the suggestion being made that it's essential we face our lack of free will.

What we *really* need to face is that we *can't face* anything in causal reality for lack of the ability to control our thoughts....

- *To realize that your mood and behavior have been caused by low blood sugar ... reveals you to be a biochemical puppet ... but it also allows you to grab hold of one of your strings ...[and] ... get a bite of food.* (Harris, p. 47)

Grabbing our strings is a metaphor for controlling ourselves and taking action. How can we do that if our behavior has been predestined and beyond our control? Grabbing our strings is exactly what determinist doctrine says we aren't capable of doing.

Determinism *is* the inability to grab our strings and influence anything.

No matter. This is *free-will speak*. Its purpose is to serve a dose of causal servitude with a spoonful of sugar.

Absent the sweetener, the only thing a determinist can say consistent with the causal faith is:

> *Causal forces can induce the belief that our mood is affected by blood sugar levels and cause us to experience "grabbing our strings" to handle the matter – but such things aren't possible in a predestined universe where we don't control our actions and have no "strings" with which to manipulate or influence anything.*

String-grabbing is advanced free will-speak.

The job of cosmic puppet-master has already been taken. The causal chain has been holding that position for 13.8 billion years and isn't showing any sign of retiring.

Until it does, there aren't any strings up for grabs.

- *If I had not decided to write this book, it wouldn't have written itself. My choice to write it was unquestionably the primary cause of its coming into being.* (Harris, p. 34)

Okay, time out!

Harris *decided* to write a book about decisions being illusory? He caused something to *come into being* that was predestined since the Big Bang?

Let us share a brief moment of silence...

How can we undertake creative activity without controlling our thoughts or actions? How can we be the *primary cause* of anything if it's already been predestined to happen just the way it must?

If Harris were to drop the *free will-speak,* he would have to say the following to abide by determinist doctrine:

> ***I was forced to "write" Free Will by causal events beyond my control. If I hadn't been, it wouldn't have written itself, but other hands might have been caused to write it. I didn't bring it "into being" because we can't bring anything into being that wasn't already predestined to come about. My "choice" to write the book wasn't the "primary cause" of anything because compelled intentions have no causal influence - let alone the ability to produce a book predestined to come into being for 13.8 billion years before I was ever born.***

I believe such reframing reveals the true nature of Harris' claim when read consistent with determinist doctrine.

But it could be I was forced to bring the sentences I just wrote into being....

Free will-speak is a powerful technology.

Who cares about a little causal bondage if we can still write books, change ourselves, make plans, rectify problems, respond intelligently, etc.?

Indeed, being determined doesn't sound any different than having the ability to choose.

Perhaps we stop arguing?...

Part Four: Is *Free Will-Speak* Shorthand?

Can the use of *free will-speak* be defended?

Isn't it just causal shorthand, a convenient way of referring to causally compelled experiences?

The "shorthand" defense doesn't work. The claim we can *unquestionably make plans, the loss of which would greatly diminish us* (p. 42), is not shorthand for what determinist doctrine maintains, namely:

> **We _un_questionably can't make plans – and _aren't_ diminished by losing a capacity we never had in the first place, and which can't exist in causal reality.**

If shorthand, *free will-speak* is a very peculiar form. Words are used to shorthand the *opposite* of what they stand for. What this is, is only shorthand for confusion.

Sunshine isn't shorthand for rain.

———

Perhaps there's a better defense: *free will-speak* must be *taken in context*. After all, it's being used by determinists whose position on such matters is eminently clear.

Most *free will-speak* claims can be stretched to comply with determinist doctrine: "we can change" doesn't literally say we're the ones *effectuating* the change. On the other hand, strained readings that comport with determinist doctrine aren't so easy to come by when it comes to claims we can "unquestionably plan", "respond intelligently", "face facts", or "rectify problems".

Who's *doing* the responding or rectifying? Who's *getting realistic* or *facing* the facts?

Context is thus no defense for *free will-speak* because it's *free will-speak* that's creating the context; a context of mixed-messages and confusion about the nature of human conduct.

Part Five: The Meditation Teacher

A respected determinist, who teaches meditation, explains that meditation can help us to:

Pay more attention, choose to follow our next thought, free our attention from trivial things, find choice points...[and] recover freedom. We have hundreds of opportunities to practice each day, can find more freedom the more we train, and have no shortage of resources we can explore.

These words, coming from a determinist?

How can we advantage from such activities if unconscious neural events determine our thoughts and actions?

Meditation seems capable of dissolving causal constraints, not just samsara. Our friendly determinist is clearly chanting a different mantra when it comes to teaching mindfulness to his students.

Oh, did I forget to mention it? The meditation instructor's name is,

Sam Harris...

Chapter Nine

LOOK WHO'S TALKING!

THE HEADLINES

Free Will and *Determined* seek to persuade its readers that free will is illusory – behavior is caused by predetermined physical events. But persuasion violates determinist doctrine – it requires the ability to direct our actions and influence what the listener thinks. Advocating for determinism can't help affirming precisely what determinist principles reject – the ability to form intentions, take deliberate actions, change what others think, and influence the world. None of these are possible if the world were predetermined – we wouldn't have the ability to control our actions and others wouldn't be capable of being influenced. To advocate for determinism is to testify against it.

Part One: Endorsing Free Will

Persuasion is an appeal to others to reconsider their point of view. It requires we author our thoughts, control our intentions, and direct our actions. It affirms our ability to influence how others think and affect their future behavior.

None of this is possible in a predestined universe where we don't control our thoughts or actions and where nothing is subject to influence.

By attempting to persuade others, determinists are engaging in actions that violate determinist doctrine.

Persuasion is a fool's errand if you're a determinist.

You can't argue on behalf of determinism without rejecting its principles.

Determinist Persuasion

The following claims illustrate the conflict between determinist doctrine and persuasion:

- **Free Will asks how we can "make sense" of our lives given the "unconscious origins" of our minds.** (p. 5)

This affirms the readers' ability to control their thoughts and the author's ability to influence them, both of which require free will and aren't possible in a world of determined behavior.

- **Harris suggests that a child murderer should be treated differently than someone who kills accidentally.** (p. 13)

This affirms the readers' ability to control their thoughts and the author's ability to change how others think – none of which is possible if our thoughts are in third party hands and our actions predestined.

- **Harris suggests the reader "appreciate" the fact that that we don't know what we intend until the intention arises.** (p. 13)

This affirms the readers' ability to control their attention, use reason, and accept an appreciative perspective – without which Harris' suggestion would makes no sense.

- ***Free Will* suggests that resignation is "extremely difficult" and challenges its readers to just try to stay in bed all day.** (p. 34)

The suggestion is largely rhetorical, but affirms that readers have the ability to actually attempt the suggested experiment. The claim it would be difficult to stay in bed all day presumes we have the ability to exercise our will and fight the temptation to end an uncomfortable condition.

- **Harris is concerned with assuaging its readers' "worry that free will is a necessary illusion" without which they can't "live creative and fulfilling lives".** (p. 45)

He's affirming he can control his actions in seeking to influence how his readers feel, which isn't possible in a predetermined world where nobody can assuage or otherwise influence anyone else.

- ***Free Will* suggests we should adopt "truths appropriate to the occasion".** (p. 46)

This concedes we have free will and can decide upon, and implement, a deliberate course of action serving our purposes.

- **Harris suggests that "getting behind" our conscious thoughts and feelings can "allow us to steer a more intelligent course".** (p. 47)

This affirms we have the capacity to freely "steer" our actions and rejects the determinist contention that we don't control what we think or do, which would mean we can't steer the course of anything.

- **Sapolsky suggests we must "face" our lack of free will. (Sapolsky, p. 391)**

This affirms we can control our thoughts, consider the consequences, and change our point of view. None of that is possible if our thoughts and behavior are determined by biology and environment. Such forces will dictate what we will face or not face, along with whatever's to follow.

Part Two: Conclusion

Persuasion is the poster-boy for free will. It isn't possible if our behavior is determined.

Hence the question: Why were *Free Will* and *Determined* written in the effort to persuade readers of the merits of determinist doctrine? Harris and Sapolsky presume their readership is capable of considering their arguments and reaching a reasoned conclusion. This isn't possible if determinism is true. They are both flagrantly violating determinist principles: you can't influence minds whose thoughts are generated by predetermined physical forces. They *aren't* subject to influence.

Recall Harris' suggestion that we're "subjugated by" the arguments we believe in. If that were the case, advocacy would be *attempted subjugation*. By such account, it's an effort to change, by way of argument, the thoughts to which someone *is presently subjugated* – and replace them with other thoughts one would prefer they be subjugated by *going forward*.

None of this works in a determined universe. Persuasion is a triply futile exercise – assuming we had the ability to control our actions and that others could control their thinking process, we you can't persuade anyone whose thoughts and behavior have already been determined. We've been preempted: the Big Bang placed everyone and everything under causal subjugation some 13.8 billion years ago. There, the story ends.

Hence when determinists seek to persuade others (writing popular books of determinist advocacy come to mind), they are violating their own doctrine. They've conceded they lack the necessary self-control for any such endeavor, and the future would have to be open, not predestined, for them to change anything.

By determinist doctrine, the Big Bang was the Big Cosmic Subjugator. There's nothing left to subjugate. The train's already left the station.

But who am I to persuade you of all this?

Chapter Ten
RESPONSIBILITY IN A CAUSAL UNIVERSE

THE HEADLINES

Harris and Sapolsky part ways on morality and personal responsibility. Harris believes they survive predetermined reality and responsibility can be assigned based on facts, never mind who's going to interpret them. He suggests we view people through the "conventional outline", pretending they have free will. Sapolsky believes the opposite - morality and personal responsibility can't be squared with predestined reality. He suggests we "face the fact" that we don't have free choice - forgetting we'd have to control our thoughts to do that, which he denies. Despite their differences, *Free Will* and *Determined* are filled with suggestions which presume free will and affirm the existence of choice, values, and judgement.

Part One: The Irreconcilable Conflict

The most difficult problem confronting determinism is how to justify the existence of moral responsibility in a world where nobody controls their thoughts or actions.

It doesn't seem possible. How could anyone be responsible for actions they don't control and can't prevent? By determinist reasoning, our actions are forced upon us by outside causal forces and we can't do otherwise. If that's the case, what could personal responsibility even mean?

The existence of morality and moral truth is equally problematic. Our beliefs are fundamentally byproducts of causal events. What we think about right and wrong is dictated by unthinking causal forces – forces that *have no conception of what morality is,* let alone how to assess moral responsibility. There is no moral truth in a causal universe – what we think is moral or immoral is whatever causal forces dictate.

Even if we could find a credible source of moral guidance in a predetermined universe, how could we follow its prescriptions if we don't control our actions?

Conceding the Problem

Virtually all determinists concede the problem:

I cannot hold you responsible for behaviors that you could not possibly control. (p. 59)

If our actions are causal events like weather patterns, how can we coherently speak about right and wrong or good and evil? (p. 48)

[In causal reality] we can no longer locate a plausible hook upon which to hang our conventional notions of responsibility. (p.17)

Despite these admissions, determinists generally insist that causal reality leaves room for both personal responsibility and moral constraints.

They seek to have it both ways.

Having Your Causal Cake

It's hard to understand why there's any dispute.

The concept of personal responsibility would seem to require we control our actions. Without such capability, we are no more responsible for our own behavior than that of the president of China. To the *very same degree*, we can't control either.

Needless to say, we lead our lives with the conviction that personal responsible exists and moral principles apply. That doesn't mean it's true. But we don't consider people responsible for what they do with a gun to their head.[1] Under determinist doctrine, we *always* have a gun to our head – the gunpoint of *predestined causal forces*.

Hence the notion of moral responsibility flies in the face of common sense. Whether by steel or by synapse, it bends credulity to think we could be responsible for causally compelled thoughts and physically induced actions.

Harris maintains that morality and personal responsibility survive a causal universe. He contends that we can assign personal responsibility "with reference to the facts".

The problem is, the facts don't speak for themselves. Indeed, by determinist principles, what we believe about "the facts" are whatever we're *caused to believe* about them.

So much for facts.

Sapolsky takes the other fork in the road.

He doesn't believe moral responsibility can be reconciled with a predetermined universe and makes no predestined bones about it:

> *Because the world is deterministic, there can't be free will, and thus holding people morally responsible is not okay. (p. 11-12)*

> *There's no such thing as free will, and blame and punishment are without any ethical justification. (page 375)*

determinist principles: making use of the conventional outline requires employment of conscious intention and deliberate purpose..

- We can't organize our thoughts if we don't control them.

- We can't ignore the deep causes of behavior and focus on the conventional outline if we don't control where we direct our attention.

- We can't increase our understanding of human nature if that understanding is compelled by causal forces predestined at the Big Bang.

- Free will can't be used as a *tool* because tools help accomplish something, and whatever we're going to accomplish or fail to achieve has already been predetermined.

Ignoring, focusing, serving, organizing, and *using tools* – these activities require the exercise of free will and have no place in the world which Harris and Sapolsky contemplate, a world where:

> *[T]he future is set – and this includes all our future states of mind and our subsequent behavior". (p. 30)*

The future state of *determinist* minds have clearly been "set" to deny the conflict between responsibility and predestiny....

How to See Others "As People"

So how do we use the "conventional outline" and apply fictive descriptions to mechanical behavior?

Harris demonstrates how pretending can yield us personal responsibility with the case of a gambler who loses his life savings playing poker:

> *To say that someone freely chose to squander his life savings at the poker table is to say that he had every opportunity to do otherwise and that nothing about what he did was inadvertent. He played poker not by accident but because he wanted to, intended to, and decided to, moment after moment. (p. 60)*

Harris' description uses free will terms to introject free will activity into what he claims is a causal universe.

To say that someone "freely choose" cannot mean what Harris' quote claims. Every assertion in the quote is a violation of determinist doctrine:

"Every opportunity to do otherwise"

He didn't have any opportunities. They don't exist in causal reality. *Determinism means* we can't do otherwise, in which case we have no opportunity to do so. The gambler can't be responsible for not taking opportunities which don't exist and he never had.

Actions weren't "inadvertent"

They were *all* inadvertent. It can't be otherwise if he didn't control his actions. *Determinism means* that no actions we take *are* advertent. He can't be responsible for actions beyond his control – which is *what* inadvertent actions *are*.

Didn't play "by accident"

There *are no* accidents in causal reality because everything is predetermined. Nothing is accidental *or* intentional in causal reality – everything unfolds as it must, not by accident; and nobody has any say in what unfolds. To say the gambler didn't play by accident suggests he did so intentionally, neither of which applies to causal reality.

"Wanted, intended, and decided to" gamble

These claims are can't be true if our thoughts are causal byproducts. The gambler's wants, intentions and decisions *weren't his* – they were causally compelled experiences forced upon him without his consent and he couldn't have experienced otherwise. His wants etc. are causal effects without influence, and without the ability to *influence anything* there's no grounds for personal responsibility.

Free Will's descriptions thus bear no resemblance to causal reality. They refer to phenomena which don't exist in a causal universe and characterize behavior in terms that presume the operation of choice.

An accurate description for the gambling scenario consistent with determinist principles would be:

> **Causal forces induced his desire to gamble and compelled him join a game. He was predestined to play until he lost his life savings. His actions were dictated by causal forces and he had no opportunity to do otherwise. He was causally compelled to "squander" his live savings and there was nothing he could do about it.**

The "conventional outline" presumes that reality can be influenced by human activity. Determinist doctrine rejects the possibility.

Seeing people *as people* in a universe of determined behavior *is pretending*. Playing make believe is no basis for morality, responsibility, or social contract based on integrity and truth.

Seeing people *as people* does nothing but prevent us from seeing causal reality *as causal*.

Part Three: When Are We Responsible?

What about our own responsibility?

Harris also has a workaround for holding *ourselves* responsible. He redirects the question of responsibility away from whether we were in control of our actions, to whether our present actions are consistent with our past:

> *To say that I was responsible for my behavior is simply to say that what I did was sufficiently in keeping with my thoughts, intentions, beliefs, and desires to be considered an extension of them. (p. 49)*

Harris offers a fanciful example:

He imagines "finding himself" running around a market naked, attempting to steal anchovies. Were that to happen, he'd find his behavior "totally out of character". He'd not consider himself "in his right mind" or "responsible" for his actions (p. 49).

But what's behind that consideration? Under determinism, nothing but mechanical thoughts forced upon him by predetermined forces. Why would Harris be any more or less responsible for parading around the market as mother nature intended than for the most noble of actions of the highest personal integrity and propriety?

By determinist terms, winning a Nobel prize isn't any more honorable or praiseworthy than running around a market naked as a baby's born.

It's all the same in causal reality. Nobody is ever in their "right mind" because all states of mind are causal effects. There's no basis on which to consider a causally induced state of mind "right", or "wrong". It's just what it is, a predestined causal byproduct. Everyone is always in whatever state of mind they were predestined to be in. End of story.

To paraphrase Dimitri in Dostoyevsky's *Brothers' Karamazov*,

In a determined universe, everything is permitted.

And that's regardless of who's got their clothes on and who doesn't.

Jeffrey Dahmer was acting in accordance with his "overall mental complexion" by luring men from bars, drugged them, strangled them, engaged in sexual activities with their corpses, and took their genitalia as souvenirs.

Ted Bundy similarly acted in character when he lured, kidnapped, raped, bludgeoned to death, and dismembered the bodies of teenage girls, one after the other.

Perfectly in character. They pass the overall mental complexion test. Fully sane, rational, responsible adults? Or mentally ill psychopaths? There's no distinction between these under the mental complexion test.

Harris' formula ignores the most recognized legal criteria for responsibility under Western jurisprudence:

Awareness of consequences, ability to know right from wrong, control over one's actions, and lack of mental or physical impairment or coercion.[2]

Would Harris be in his "right mind" if his daily exercise regimen consisted of running around naked at supermarkets? By his own terms, you bet. Frightful thought? Readers are left to their own thought experiment.... Author, agnostic.

Harris' character test fundamentally contradicts determinist principles: nobody ever controls what they do in a causal universe, *whether their actions are in character or not.*

I believe I'm in my "right mind" in saying this.

If it helps you to assess this, I don't like anchovies and I don't think I'm naked.

Part Four: When Are Others Responsible?

Undaunted, Harris suggests that we can find a "notion of personal responsibility that fits the facts" (p. 49).

It suggests five hypothetical cases of gunshot deaths to illustrate *relative degrees* of responsibility:

Child's Play

A young child accidentally discharges a gun while playing and kills someone. Free Will says we don't consider the child responsible as the killing wasn't "on purpose". (p. 51) But nobody is capable of killing anyone on purpose in causal reality. Guns discharge when predestined, no matter in whose hand. Harris is deferring to free will values:

Limited grasp of circumstances dampens or precludes the capacity for free will.

Taunted Teenager

A young teenager, abused as a child, shoots someone teasing him. Free Will says he's less responsible than a "fully mature" adult, his intentions don't "run as deep". (pp. 50-51)

But nobody is responsible for their actions in causal reality, no matter how "mature", which they don't control in any case. Harris is deferring to free will values:

Limited maturity reduces the capacity for self-control and exercise of choice.

Jilted Lover

An adult male, abused as a child, shoots his ex-girlfriend for leaving him. Free Will says his guilt is mitigated because it's a "crime of passion", driven by overwhelming emotion influenced by childhood abuse. (pp. 50-51) But emotions are causal byproducts and childhood trauma is predestined. They didn't cause pulling the trigger which was equally and always predestined. Harris is deferring to free will values:

Overwhelming emotion compromises the ability to choose rationally and control one's behavior.

Psychopath

An adult, who had a happy childhood, shoots someone "for the fun of it". Free Will says his motives "brand him a psychopath", presumably meaning he was acting from mental dysfunction and not responsible for the shooting. (p. 50) But childhood history and bizarre declarations are passive causal effects which had no influence on his pulling the trigger – they were always predestined to occur. Harris is deferring to free will values:

Extreme and bizarre conduct reflects the inability to act rationally and exercise control over one's actions.

Tumor Victim

Same adult as in the last example, but with massive brain tumor. Free Will says that physical influence negates his responsibility. (pp. 50-51) But all behavior is determined in a causal universe, whether related to dysfunction or otherwise. Harris concedes elsewhere that a tumor is but one example of brain activity "giving rise to thoughts and actions" (p. 5). Harris is deferring to free will values:

Neural impairment compromises the capacity for choice and the ability to control one's actions.

Criteria for Responsibility

Determinism is the great leveler.

It provides no basis on which to assign responsibility because nobody controls their actions. The factors called upon in *Free Will's* examples have one thing in common:

They measure *the degree to which one's exercise of free will is compromised.*

Without the ability to choose, factors such as age, childhood, emotional turmoil, tumors, etc. don't mean anything with respect to personal or social accountability. Ranking relative degrees of responsibility isn't possible when nobody has any responsible for anything *in the first place.*

Biochemical robots aren't responsible for following what their biochemical programming dictates.

It's the only thing they *can* do.

Part Five: Well-Being

Two years prior to *Free Will*, Harris published a book called *The Moral Landscape*.[3]

Moral good is equated with maximizing the "well-being" of conscious creatures (p. 14). This is a contemporary take on the utilitarian directive – the greatest good for the greatest number.

Harris' suggestion that we should maximize well-being contradicts determinist principles. The moral injunction to increase well-being requires the ability to form intentions, take action, and influence the unfolding of reality – all of which are rejected by determinist doctrine.

The concept of *well-being* can't have any moral significance in a causal universe. Acting to increase well-being is no more or less virtuous than mass murder. Our actions our causally compelled no matter what they may be. And whatever we think virtuous is whatever we're caused to believe.

To think this isn't the case confuses the nature of causal reality, which doesn't serve anyone's well-being....

Part Six: The Justice System

Harris refuses to dispense with social justice, however inconsistent it may be with determinist reality:

Certain criminals must be incarcerated...the moral justification for this is straightforward: Everyone else will be better off this way. (p. 53)

The claim is based on free will values and requires free will abilities to be implemented. Neither exist in a causal universe. We value whatever we're caused to value. (If you don't value *this* explanation, perhaps you weren't meant to...)

In a determined world, there is no justification for the pillars on which Western jurisprudence and justice are based – equal treatment, procedural fairness, containment of bias, judgement by peers, right of appeal, etc. These have value only if we're caused to believe they do.

It's said that justice is blind.

This is especially so if it's generated by unthinking causal forces – forces so blind as to have no conception of what justice means in the first place.

Sapolsky's recipe for justice violates determinist doctrine from the gate. He favors the "quarantine model", which is the "logical and morally acceptable" approach:

> *A car that, through no fault of its own, has brakes that don't work should be kept off the road. A person with active COVID-19, through no fault of their own, should be blocked from attending a crowded concert. A leopard that would shred you, through no fault of its own, should be barred from your home. (Sapolsky, p. 347)*

These are reasonable suggestions. But each the undertaking of deliberate actions. If behavior is determined and our actions "the outcome of the second before, minutes before, millennia before" (p. 123), who's capable of taking deliberate actions to accomplish such purposeful goals? Who's going to take broken cars off the road? Who's going to block Covid-19 patients from crowds? Who's going to enact legislation to prevent adopting wild animals, such as leopards, as domestic pets?

Sapolsky's recommendations thus violate determinist principles by presupposing the ability to form intentions and control our actions. If our behavior is determined by prior conditions, people will follow his advice *if it was predetermined* "seconds before", minutes before", etc. If not, they won't. It's not up to whom he's appealing. Either way, he's wasting his predetermined breath.

Moral and Cultural Relativism

Numerous cultures engage in practices that shock our sense of morality and common decency.

Some societies endorse trial by jury. Others throw adulterers off rooftops. Some societies require due process before determining guilt or innocence. Others cut off hands without trial or further ado.

No moral distinctions among these are possible under determinist doctrine. Social values and practices are the product of blind causal forces. No culture has any privileged position when it comes to moral truth. Indeed, the belief that one's cultural practices reflect greater moral integrity *is itself* a causally compelled belief.

Whether forgiveness or decapitation, whether rehabilitation or torture – cultural practices are causal byproducts under determinist doctrine. None of them have the moral high ground over any other.

Moral relativism is unavoidable when all beliefs about moral truth are equally the causal byproducts of unthinking physical activities.

Part Seven: Conclusion

How to square the notion of responsibility and morality in a world of causally compelled behavior? Both concepts appear to conflict with core determinist principles:

Responsibility implies control over one's actions, and morality implies standards of conduct that can't be derived from the causal activity of physical events.

The attempt to reconcile such notions leads to unavoidable contradiction – responsibility is demanded of causally compelled behavior, and morality is demanded of thoughts dictated by unthinking physical events. What could responsibility and morality possibly mean under such circumstances?

Harris believes objective standards can solve the problem The moral project is about maximizing well-being; the means therefor provided by reason, knowledge, and science. The moral propriety of conduct can be measured by applying the "conventional outline" – by assuming what determinism denies, that we have free will and should be held accountable for our conduct. Borrowing standards from a world in which choice exists avoids the problem: why the need to call upon free will principles to salvage morality and responsibility?

The question answers itself. If you don't presume the existence of choice, there's no way to assess moral responsibility. The two-fold problem is ignored by Sapolsky and Harris:

What *values* are going to be used for the assessment? Physical processes can't provide them.

And what *justifies* pretending we have free will in order to solve the problem? Harris has no answers, other than practical purposes. But practical purposes require *deliberate actions;* that we *control our behavior.* Suddenly it seems we have such abilities after all. Hence we're back to square one.

Sapolsky bites the bullet. We can pretend all we want, but responsibility and morality can't be squared with determined behavior. Let's just fess up. But having done so, he proceeds to prescribe actions which, notwithstanding the conflict, presume we have choice and affirm our ability to abide by moral standards. He thus ends up in the same place as Harris. Both propose "solutions" which require adopting intentions and taking deliberative action, for which we *have no capacity* in causal reality – assessing future risks, protecting people from harm, addressing the root causes of crime, scrapping notions of blame and punishment for quarantine practice, and incarcerating criminals knowing we may do so with "straightforward moral justification".

How can these be squared with causal reality, when each of these prescriptions flatly reject determinist precepts and depend on the ability to control thoughts and direct actions?

Hence we're left without any coherent theory of moral responsibility *based on determinist principles* and *consistent with determinist doctrine.*

Harris thinks he has surmounted the problem. Sapolsky, less so. In the end, both fail to concede that their suggestions flatly contradict determinist premises. Their recommendations avoid, rather than resolve, the fundamental conflict:

- *In a world where we can't choose, control, or avoid doing what we're causally compelled to undertake, how are we to follow the social injunctions which Harris and Sapolsky commend to us?*

- *Without control over our thoughts or actions, how could we intend, reason, assess, judge, protect, remedy, and take deliberate action in service of their commendations with "straightforward moral justification"?*

- *Where are the values and principles coming from by which Harris and Sapolsky purport to justify their recommended social policies and practices? If all our thoughts - including our beliefs about morality and personal responsibility - are generated by predestined causal forces, including biology and environment, how can physical events produce "straightforward moral justifications" based on moral principles?*

In the end, Harris' and Sapolsky's social prescriptions violate the principle tenets of determinist doctrine. They lack foundation or justification in a mechanical universe comprised of physical forces and causally compelled beliefs.

What could the greater good mean to a quark?

Chapter Eleven
KNOWING WHY

THE HEADLINES

Harris claims we can't have free will because we lack the ability to explain our actions - we can only give after-the-fact "stories". The claim confuses reasons with choice. Reasons influence choices but don't require them. There are often good reasons for choosing more than one alternative. If it exists, deliberative choice is based on valuing reasons and acting accordingly. Construing explanations as "stories" is circular - it would only be the case were determinism presumed true and our actions caused by unthinking events - which render reasons and explanation irrelevant. Absent such presumption, adequate explanations are available for any type of decision which, by nature, calls for one.

Part One: Why We Do Things?

We usually know why we do things.

At least we think we do, and under most circumstances are certain of it. Harris argues otherwise. He insists we don't have a clue as to why we do things; and can't have free will if we *don't know why* we behave as we do.

> *Our thoughts and behaviors are mysteries. (p. 43) I could tell a story about why I'm doing what I'm doing... but the actual explanation is hidden from me. (pp. 43-44)*

We may think we're explaining things, but we're just telling after the fact "stories".

> *You might have a story to tell... but it would be nothing more than a post-hoc decision. You might be able to tell a story...but you cannot truly account for why you let it happen. (p. 35, 37)*

The argument makes some sense.

If we don't know why we do things, how can we do them deliberately? Even when we're most confident in our reasons, we don't know what we're talking about – we are *always* mistaken about the true causes of our behavior.

Harris offers the following examples:

- *Harris chooses coffee over tea, but is "in no position to know [why]." (p. 7)*

- *Harris resumed martial arts inspired by a book on violence, but has "no idea" why he found it compelling. (pp. 43-44)*

- *Someone fails to turn their life around. A year later they succeed, but "can't know why" they were able to this time. (p. 39)*

Explanations don't seem that elusive.

I get gas because I don't want to run out. I deposit the check so that I have money in my account. I check my calendar each morning so that I know who to blow off before I start doing whatever I want.

What's wrong with these reasons?

Nothing, but they conflict with the premise that our behavior is determined, by which reasons don't factor into why we do things. By circular reasoning, Harris insists we do them because causal forces make us and reasons are thus irrelevant:

- **We don't have free will because we can't explain our actions.**

- *We can't explain our actions because they are caused by physical forces, not reasons.*

Absent determinist presumptions, there's no reason to construe explanations as stories.

If you think otherwise, don't get gas the next time you need it and see what happens.

Trust me, *that* will be a story....

Part Two: Decisions and Reasons

The *knowing why* argument confuses decisions and reasons. There are many different kinds of decisions. Some require reasons, some don't. None of them are compelled by reason alone. That's not what reasons *are*.

Reasons *influence* the choices we make, to a greater or lesser degree – but they don't dictate the choices to which they pertain. That's not their function.

Rudimentary actions aside, decisions are about deliberating, *valuing* reasons, and committing to act accordingly. There are usually good reasons for multiple alternatives. A choice is about what we *value most*, all things considered.

> *We often have to resolve conflicts between self-regarding motives and other-regarding motives....An important aspect of plausible*

reasoning is that it apparently enables us to reach decisions that resolve conflicting reasons, which are of different types and cannot be explicitly compared on a common scale.[1]

In short, reasons *don't make choices*.

Moreover, different types of decisions call for different types of explanations. If we can't find a reason for a choice whose nature requires one, it's usually because we're looking for the wrong kind of reason in the wrong place.

Types of Explanations

Explanations can loosely be divided into two kinds, *causal* and *purposeful*.

Causal explanations refer to prior physical events. *Purposeful* explanations refer to reasons, motivations, or purposes.

Determinists favors causal explanations because they align with determinist principles. They match one physical event to another. As a result, they are often circular.

Determinists reject *purposeful* explanations for the same reason they embrace *causal* ones. It's not for lack of explanatory ability, but because *purposeful* explanations assume *purposeful* actions, which in turn assume *purposeful* intentions and decisions.

Types of Decisions

It's also important to distinguish amongst types of decisions. Broadly speaking, there are three kinds: *practical, preference-based,* and those which seem *arbitrary*.

- *Practical decisions* are easily explained because they concern a means to an end. *I grabbed the hammer to drive in the nail. I used a stamp because I wanted the mail to get there.*

- *Preference-based decisions* are explained by reference to matters of taste, preference, and subjective factors. *I ordered chocolate because I like it. I don't want to meet up with him because he's more boring than a brick wall.*

- *Arbitrary decisions* (which only seem so) are explained by context. *You pick a number between one and ten at a magic how. You like chocolate and vanilla cupcakes equally, but can choose only one.*

The Problem With Practical Decisions

Determinists don't want to mess with practical decisions. It's dangerous to go there. Such decisions, by nature, have iron-clad explanations. They concern specific means to purposeful, articulated ends. They have ready explanations, whether the choice itself is wise or not.

The *knowing why* argument breaks down when practical decisions are considered. Harris must thus turn elsewhere to demonstrate our inability to explain our actions. The focus is thereby directed to *preference-based* decisions, and those involving *arbitrary factors*.

But these, too, have rational explanations. One must look for them in the right place to find the type of explanation that befits their nature.

Preference-Based Decisions

Yes, I like chocolate ice cream!

Who knows why? I *just do*. It's a subjective preference. But the reason why I'm about to order a hot fudge Sunday isn't. The reason is indisputable: I order it *because I like it.* There's nothing arbitrary about that.

Lurking behind every preference-based decision is a *utilitarian*[2] explanation. *Because I like it* is one of the most informed, rational, and sound explanations there is. It's backed by empirical evidence and based on sound reasoning:

- **It's a fact** - chocolate delivers a most pleasurable sensation whenever it comes into contact with my taste buds.

- **It's a fact** – there's a 100% correlation between that sensation and cocoa-tongue contact, objectively verified under many different conditions.

- **It's a fact** - we are pleasure seeking creatures motivated by seeking conditions that replicate prior pleasurable experiences.

Decisions about preferences and desires involve subjective factors – but *it's the factors* that are arbitrary, not the choice taking them into account.

At their core, preference-based decisions are practical, of utility for satisfying some need or desire.

Preferences are *conditions,* which for the most part we don't choose to have. They are *internal* conditions. We must take them as they are. Forks in the road are *external* conditions. We must also take those as they are. No matter the kind, conditions constrain free will but there's no reason to believe they preclude it. They are part of the landscape of circumstances that provide conditions, which in turn provide us with alternatives.

You can turn right or left at the fork regardless of whether you constructed the highway.

My craving for chocolate doesn't prevent me from ordering carrots instead.

That said, I'll stick with the fudge....

Arbitrary Magic

"Arbitrary" decisions only seem so.

You stand up at a magic show and are asked to pick a number. You call out number 4. Why not 6?

You have no idea why.

It doesn't matter. It's not the relevant question. The nature of the request required you to call out something arbitrary, something random. That was a *limiting condition* contained in the request for which you volunteered. The condition was provided by the context.

Supplying a random factor didn't stop you from volunteering, standing up, selecting a number, and calling it out for the audience. It didn't stop you from considering the various numbers that popped into your head and selecting one. By appealing to random mental activity, you achieved the purpose you set out to accomplish:

You took your kids to a magic show and made it extra fun for them by having mommy participate.

The number was random, not the actions you took to come up with it or the reasons why you did so.

There's no magic about why you stood up and shouted out a number....

———

Harris offers the same type of example in his *Final Thoughts on Free Will* podcast. He asks his audience to pick a movie, any movie. He challenges them to explain why they "stopped on the one [they] chose".

It's a trick question. Due to determinist presumptions, there *is no* rational explanation he'll find acceptable. There *is no* explanation for why arbitrary elements appear in any given situation. That's why they're *arbitrary*. But they pose a challenge for free will only if they're *abstracted from the context* – i.e., if one ignores the purpose for his request in the first place, and the rational sequence of events necessitated by anyone who wishes to comply.

Asking for someone to call out a movie they've seen requires they accept the invitation, call upon memory, and make a selection amongst the alternatives that come to mind. The selection may be arbitrary, but not *the act of selection*. That has a purpose. Given the context, there's nothing arbitrary about it.

There's no reason why the selection of an arbitrary element, which isn't susceptible to rational explanation, should make *the choice itself* arbitrary. Harris offers no explanation (or after-the-fact story) for why it should.

The exercise proposed by Harris *presupposes* free will. It would be meaningless, devoid of purpose were his audience incapable of controlling their thoughts and actions. His appeal thus violates determinist premises. Consider what he'd have to say to his audience were he to attempt consistency with determinist doctrine:

> *I am going to suggest a thought experiment which I was predestined to suggest. You are going to respond to it however you were*

predetermined to react. Afterwards, I'm going to offer what I've been predestined to explain to you about its meaning. You're then going to accept that explanation or reject it, depending on what position you've been predestined to adopt.

Suppose, instead, Harris had asked his audience to:

Think of a movie you would never show to your five-year old son and select one.

Now we have a different ballgame.

The question implicates purposes, reason, and values. Something's now *at stake*. That an audience member wouldn't likely choose *Midnight Cowboy* for their child is no longer anything arbitrary. And the fact that they could have chosen *Taxi Driver, Apocalypse Now,* or *Debbie Does Dallas* instead doesn't make it their choice of *Mary Poppins* arbitrary.

In sum, Harris seeks to discredit free will by abstracting isolated random elements from the context in which they appear, thus obscuring the purpose, deliberation, and actions that arise in response to a context in which arbitrary factors happen to be involved.

One might say with good cause that it's an arbitrary way to look at it....

Part Three: Essential Knowledge

Harris argues that free will would require other knowledge besides explanations for our actions.

We would also need to know:

- *Our next thought*

- *Our next mental state*

- *The alternatives*

- *Why we succeed when we do*

Our Next Thought

What are you going to think next?

If you don't know, you're out of luck. Harris maintains that such lack of foreknowledge disqualifies you from freely thinking it when the time arrives to do so:

I cannot decide what I will next think or intend until a thought or intention arises. (p. 9)

If you don't know what your soul is going to do next, you are not in control. (p. 12)

What will my next mental state be? I don't know, it just happens. Where is the freedom in that? (p. 9)

If these claims seem counter-intuitive, it's because they don't accurately reflect how thinking works:

Linear Thinking

Thinking takes place linearly and we can only think what we're thinking in the moment. We'll think our next thought when it comes time to think it.

Nothing is Next Until It's Next

Our next thought doesn't become our next thought until the moment we think it. If we knew what it was going to be, that would be a present thought.

Knowing The Future

We can't know our next thought because it doesn't yet exist. Until we think it, there's nothing to know.

Last Moment Changes

Our next thought is always subject to last moment change prompted by sudden occurrences, interruptions, new ideas, etc. Such influences don't cease until the moment we think it.

Sapolsky expands upon Harris' *knowing-your-next-thought* argument.

> *Sam Harris argues convincingly that it's impossible to successfully think of what you're going to think next. The takeaway from [prior chapters] is that it's impossible to successfully wish what you're going to wish for. It's impossible to successfully will yourself to have more willpower. Page 124*

The same objections apply. Until we wish something we haven't yet begun to wish for, there's nothing to know. Until we exert our will, there's no telling what obstacles we will encounter, internal and external. The universe unfolds in successive temporal moments and while we can speculate all we wish, we can't know for certain what thoughts or behavior are going to be before they occur. There's nothing yet *to know*.

Given the nature of time and the temporal nature of the thinking process, this isn't evidence against free will:

It's evidence against *clairvoyance*.

Our Next Mental State

Harris also claims that having free will would require knowing our next mental state before the fact.

Personally speaking, I'd rather not know most of them even after they've arrived, let alone before…

But as with decisions, states of mind are the product of many factors. Mood, attention level, circumstances, mental framework, urgency, amount of sleep, chemical balance, mental dysfunction, etc. Until the factors combine to generate that state, it doesn't exist and there's *nothing to know*.

The stew can't be tasted until the ingredients are combined and cooked.

That doesn't mean there's no chef in the kitchen.

Accounting for Success

Free Will asks us to imagine our "life has gone off track". We've tried without success to "escape this downward trend" and gave up. A year later we tried again and this time met with success.

> *Why did you encounter so many obstacles in yourself [the first-time round]? You have no idea. (p. 35)*

Why would you not know that? Absent unusual conditions, there's no reason this should be the case.

Another year of experience is a long time. It allows new skills, knowledge, and resources to be harnessed. We usually know what formerly worked against us and what new advantages we had thereafter.

Each attempt we make to accomplish something involves a different climber scaling a different mountain. This betters the odds of succeeding in subsequent efforts.

We don't always succeed. But it's almost always the explanation for why….

Knowing the Alternatives

Free Will suggests that choice requires we know all the available alternatives.

> *Why did I not decide to drink a glass of juice? The thought never occurred to me. Am I free to do that which does not occur to me to do? Of course not. (p. 19)*

Harris makes the same point in his pick-a-movie exercise.[3] We can't have chosen the *Wizard of Oz* if we didn't think of it, because our "*Wizard of Oz* circuits were not in play" when we were making the choice.

He is right. We can't choose an alternative we don't know about. This says *nothing* about free will: that our choices are limited by our knowledge proves only that our choices are limited, that's all. Not that they don't exist within the confines of what we *do* know.

We can always order off a menu that's missing the last two pages.

We just have to order from the pages *that are there*.

Part Four: Conclusion

Reasons aren't choices.

They influence our decisions, but don't require we make them. There's often compelling reasons behind more than one alternative. The choice is about committing to one of them.

But this is all beside the point: in a determined universe, there's *no such thing* as reasons. They *don't exist*. This is the hidden premise behind the Harris' *knowing why* argument:

In a mechanical universe, reasons are *causally induced thoughts* which don't influence behavior, which is driven solely by causal forces that *don't operate with regard to reason or explanation.*

Explanations are "stories" under determinist doctrine, because they have no bearing on causally compelled behavior. In other words, they are *after the fact* stories – but *only if* viewed through the *before the fact* presumption that determinism is true.

Predetermined Postscript

These thoughts suggest another causal Koan for contemplation:

Can a determinist explain why explanations are after-the-fact stories without giving yet another after-the-fact story?

Chapter Twelve
OBSERVATION AND ENGAGEMENT

THE HEADLINES

Harris offers a unique experiential argument against free will: since we don't control our thoughts we can't author them - we passively watch them arise before our minds, parading by as we observe them from the bleachers. The argument is based on what experience discloses, but selectively chooses the experiences best suited to make the case. Other routine experiences in our daily lives are ignored - along with neuroscience's recognition that diverse streams of thought exhibit different neural characteristics of differing meaning and implication. Introspective observation comes in more than one flavor. Harris' observation argument is based on experiential cherry-picking.

Part One: Watching Thoughts Arise

Harris turns to experience to make the determinist case against choice. But he does so selectively.

Harris offers introspective experience as evidence we don't author our thoughts. When we introspect, we passively watch them arise from somewhere outside consciousness, as if "from the void" (p.34). We can't "trace" such thoughts "to any point of origin" in our minds. (p. 6)

For Harris, introspection is the only game in town[1]:

We don't create our thoughts, they simply arise unauthored. (p. 32)

Where did this idea ... come from? It just appeared in your mind. (p. 37)

Thoughts and intentions simply arise in the mind. (p. 64)

To be sure, introspection suggest we don't originate our thoughts. But that's *just introspection* – it isn't the only type of experience we have. By contrast, we can engage in a thinking process in which we experience actively originating and managing our thoughts. We calculate, problem solve, gather facts, consider options, weigh strategies, organize matters, etc. We aren't spectators watching a ceaseless thought parade from the sidelines – we are leading the band and directing the march.

If we're looking to experience, we must consider what different types of experiences disclose. Contrary to what introspection suggests, engaged thinking appears to offer experiential validation of our capacity for choice. Looking to experience thus renders a split decision – whether we control our thoughts or are controlled by them is a function of *which experience* is being called upon.

Naturally, experiences overlap and interweave amongst each other. There's a natural and seamless ebb and flow amongst them from moment to moment.

> *When I am writing something, ideas are thrown up by unconscious processes; but I am continually appraising the sense and sound of chunks of what I am writing so as to decide whether to keep them or to alter them or to try and come up with other ideas. My actions seemed to flow from an ongoing process with complementary contributions from unconscious processes and conscious experiences.*[2]

Some experiences put us on the bench watching the game. Others put us out there on the playing field in the middle of the action.

Experience suggests we can do both, as befits the occasion.

Harris and Sapolsky wrote books *inviting us* to get off the bench and into the game. They've asked us to hear them out. If we're *not* determinists, they're asking us to reconsider the merits of determinist doctrine. If we *are* determinists, they're out to reinforce our conviction that we've got it right.

They're engaging us in an active thinking process. We are called upon to direct attention, control thoughts, evaluate evidence, judge arguments, and reaching a conclusion based on all things considered. They're not asking us to kick back and watch our thoughts arise and float on by.

At least, those are my thoughts floating on by...

Authentic, or Illusory?

The *thoughts arising* argument looks to experience for evidence against free will, but selectively. Nothing found in the experience of introspection or engaged thinking provides any basis by which to distinguish their relative authenticity. We experience them as equally genuine.

Harris offers no criteria by which to make any such distinction. The selective emphasis on introspection appears attributable to its fit within the determinist narrative. His argument thus begs the question:

- **We don't author our thoughts because we passively watch them arise.**

- *We passively watch them arise because our thoughts are determined and we have no control over what arises.*

Using the determinist overlay to pick and choose among experiences on which to base metaphysical conclusions doesn't pass experiential muster.

Part Two: The Neuroscience Findings

Observation and engaged thinking are experiential bookends. One appears passive, the other active. But there's no bright line between them and each intrinsically depends on the other.

Engaged thinking governs problem solving, calculating, strategizing, etc. – but ideas and insights that arise before our minds as we engage in such activities fuel the process. Conversely, introspection governs meditation, contemplation, self-awareness, memory, etc. – but intentions, concerns, and values influence what "arises" are an integral part of such processes.

Meditation starts with the intention to meditate. We call upon knowledge for procedure and technique. The practice involves directing attention, monitoring, adjusting, etc. – all in service of remaining watchful and purposely engaging the meditative process.

Meditation is an active, intentional process – it's *actively engaging* in *passive disengagement*. Part purpose, part surrender.

But there's nothing unique about that. We are constantly calling upon thoughts to arise – a process in which we actively define their parameters to serve our intentions and purposes.

> *You perform actions...querying a memory system with a certain kind of probe, called a retrieval set.... And content addressable memory works its magic. It delivers the answer to your query. You agentially perform the catalytic action and passively receive the result of the kind of thing you're after.[3]*

From creative ventures to problem solving, we engage in "catalytic action" – surrendering to what arises, observing what comes up, and evaluating what best suits the occasion. We reject what doesn't work and modify what we think could work after some adjustment.

Contrary to Harris' partial description, thoughts don't arise "as though from the void" independent of intention, purpose, or significance. Even when we daydream, our thought streams are steeped in meaningful and purposeful concerns:

> *SST (spontaneous streams of thought) is decisional, with propositional and computational structure richly imbued with agency, stay-go decisions, elaboration decisions, and the like. Your personal concerns and what's important to you manifests through these...decisions.*

Neuroscience findings challenge Harris' thought observation argument. Conscious states are interwoven with each other without clear lines of demarcation.

> *Meta-analysis that summarizes neuroimaging literature on mental categories such as emotion, memory, etc. confirm that brain regions show little psychological specificity...mental states emerge from the combination of domain general psychological processes ... that map to large-scale distributed networks in associated regions of the brain.*[4]

Even meditation, watchful as it is of thoughts arising, is no exception. More than a few things are going on when we cross our legs like the Buddha and kick back for a daily dose of enlightenment:

> *No matter which... style of mindfulness practice we choose...[it] consists in the integrated exercise of a host of cognitive, affective, and bodily skills in situated action. To conceive of meditation as a kind of private introspection is wrong. It ... is not inner perception of [a] ... private mental realm; rather it is metacognition... of socially constituted experience.*[5]

According to neuroscience, meditation isn't entirely that meditative after all. Broader influences are also at play that can't be segregated from the introspective experience:

> *High-level cognitions are produced by a confluence of factors. They include cultural practices, habits of attending, and the use of bodily responses interacting with material and social surroundings.*[6]

Harris' argument presumes experiences discrete; that our thoughts randomly arise and float about free of intention, deliberation, prior decisions, purposes, values, present concerns and thoughts about what's to come.

The stream of neuroscience findings suggest otherwise.

Part Three: Is *Free Will* a Feeling?

Harris characterizes free will as a *feeling, or felt experience*. The depiction reduces choice to an arbitrary, internal experience – subjective, without substance, unrelated to reality. It's nothing to bother about.

After all…it's just a feeling….

> *Our belief in free will is "attributable to the fact that most of us feel that we freely author our own*

thoughts and actions." (p. 15) Free will "emerges from a felt experience." (p. 15)

But *feeling* refers to a vast array of experiences. Pain, happiness, bodily discomfort, intuition, substance affects, etc. – all "feelings", but different experiences with differing characteristics.

The free will "feeling" isn't of the same order. It's an immediate, in-the-moment experience of connecting and engaging the world through awareness, intention, reason, purpose, judgement, recall, and planning – intertwined with the experience of influencing reality and being influenced by it.

Labeling free will a feeling is circular, an experiential interpretation derived from determinist premises:

- **Our experience of free will is an illusory feeling.**

- **It's an illusory feeling because we are determined and don't have the ability to choose.**

In short, the feeling of free will isn't evidence for determinism. It's only a "feeling" if you presume determinism true. That's my feeling about it anyway.

Part Four: Conclusion

We're always jumping back and forth between observing, engaging, observing, engaging….

It's the yin and yang of consciousness:

There's the Ray Bradbury that writes, and the "me" that watches him. I can't believe that there are two of me, and I'm the witness now, to what I did before. And I think I am so lucky that God made me in two halves – the creator and the witness.[7]

The *thoughts arising* argument thus embraces the witness half and discards the creator, the *active "me"* that watches the *other "me"* do its thing.

From an adaptive viewpoint, this doesn't make sense. Imagine a thunderstorm gathering. Or an enemy tribe circling. Or a den of lions seen lurking about nearby. Sitting still and passively watching your thoughts arise as you hope for enlightenment doesn't seem the wisest of choices.

Vigilance, alertness, readiness for action ,and proactive strategizing would seem time better spent.

You'd be less likely to get swept away, wind up as a trophy, or become somebody's lunch.

Chapter Thirteen
WHY DOES IT MATTER?

THE HEADLINES

Harris and Sapolsky insist that there are benefits to giving up the belief in free will. Harris reports that he takes things less personally and is more forgiving of himself and others. Sapolsky believes the acceptance of determinism will end the "blame game" and will allow us to dispassionately protect society and others from danger. Both acknowledge the science findings which suggest otherwise – that the belief in determinism tends to promote aggressiveness and anti-social conduct, while the belief in free will tends to increase honesty and integrity.

Part One: Determinism and Anti-Social Conduct

Why does the free will issue matter?

There are many reasons to hope free will exists. It would allow us to control our behavior and influence our lives. It would allow us to influence others and change the course of worldly affairs. It would provide the grounds for personal and social responsibility. It would permit us to express ourselves creatively and make a difference.

That not a bad list for starters.

There's another reason perhaps less self-evident. It seems the belief in free will tends to encourage good will, integrity, honesty, and social responsibility. And that the belief in determinism tends to increase cheating, aggressiveness, and anti-social conduct.

These are pretty good reasons to hope we have the capacity to choose.

The Science

Several science studies report on how free will and determinist beliefs affect behavior. Among the most frequently cited:

- The *Vohs-Schooler* study (2008) found that "exposure to the deterministic message increased cheating. Participants who read statements endorsing free will did not [cheat]."[1]

- The *Baumeister* study (2009) found that the "induced disbelief in free will reduced willingness to help others ... and caused participants to act more aggressively than others."[2]

Yet another line of studies focuses on how our beliefs about free will affect our viewpoint about how others behave:

- The *Shariff* study (2014) indicates that the belief in determinism reduced retributive attitudes toward other people. [3]

- The *Krueger* study (2014) concludes correspondingly that people who strongly believe in free will tend to be more punitive, not less. [4]

- The *Casper* study (2017) found that "disbelief in free will had a positive impact on the morality of decisions towards others." [5]

What accounts for these findings?

Perhaps accepting that others don't choose their actions prompts more leniency – after all, people can't help themselves. And perhaps believing in free will prompts less leniency because, after all, others had the ability to act otherwise but chose not to.

Either way, fostering personal integrity and acting from the higher virtues aren't bad reasons for encouraging the belief that free will is possible.

They may be the best reasons....

Part Two: Losing the Belief in Free Will

As critics often point out, the belief that we lack control over our behavior is a ripe excuse for misconduct.

If free will is a myth, and our actions are the mere amoral outcome of biological lock... why not just run amok? "Don't blame me; I was possessed by ...the evil tiger spirit of the forest" is just a hop, skip, and jump away from "don't blame me; we are just biological machines. (p. 246)

But a more responsible attitude is also possible. Harris writes of his personal experience:

Losing a belief in free will ... has increased my feelings of freedom. My hopes, fears, and neuroses seem less personal and indelible. (p. 46)

What he's describing isn't possible if human behavior is determined. By determinist terms, the matter is academic – one has no control over what beliefs one's going to surrender or hold onto. Nor does what one believes have any influence over anything one does – all our thoughts and actions were *predetermined* for all eternity *at the same time* back when the cosmos was born. Causal forces determine what beliefs we change and what we do and don't experience thereafter.

It's all a part of the same predestined show.

Harris' change in attitude owes no more to dropping the belief in free will than it does to the bellowing of a bullfrog in China.

Part Three: Conclusion

The science studies must be put in perspective.

They are limited to artificial laboratory conditions. Subjects know well they can cheat without consequences. They are exposed to brief readings of determinist and free will advocacy. Their reactions most likely reflect temporary influence, rather than reasoned judgements or deeply held convictions.

Nor is there evidence that test-condition reactions correlate with the level of moral conduct with which subjects actually live their lives in the ordinary course. In addition, there's little more than a handful of such studies to begin with.

On the other hand, the findings align with common sense – the belief that we can't control our actions would seem more likely to encourage misconduct than the belief that we are fully responsible for what we do.

First, it was *the devil* made me do it.

Next, it was *the twinkies* made me do it.

And now, courtesy of determinist doctrine, comes the ultimate defense –

Causal forces made me do it!

Chapter Fourteen

THE GREATEST STORY EVER TOLD

Determinism is the greatest story ever told.

One of the most popular scientific theories of all time, the gospel of causation is readily embraced by scientist and layperson alike.[1] It plays to sell-out crowds worldwide and is always streaming – no "buy now" payment required.

The mark of a great story is its ability to divert audience attention from lapses of logic, drifts in plausibility, and gaps in the narrative. Determinism excels at breezing by all such foibles, and nobody's the wiser. Popular determinist advocacy gives but token scrutiny to narrative integrity.

Among its more implausible plotlines:

- ***Subplot One:*** *Science supports and justifies determinist doctrine.*

    The subplot neglects to mention that the fundamental laws of physics don't concern causation; that the genesis of causal structures and the appearance of sequential cause-effect relations remains scientifically and philosophically uncertain; and that the relevance of causation in physics and advanced sciences has been under dispute for more than a century.

- **Subplot Two:** *The universe is governed by physical events in a causal chain that started with the Big Bang.*

  The subplot fails to mention that such causal forces aren't conscious; that they don't think, reason, or deliberate. Yet they somehow manage to organize themselves into conceptual patterns based on meaning, significance, language, logic, reason, values, social hierarchies, etc. Such non-physical frameworks follow conceptual rules that aren't found in the laws of physics. Physical forces nevertheless manage to abide by such rules, arranging themselves into subatomic configurations which, <u>without the benefit of intention or foresight</u>, happen to generate telescopes, sports arenas, airplanes, and the collected works of Shakespeare.

- **Subplot Three**: *Human behavior is generated by neural reactions shaped by the collective causal* *influence of biology, environment, personal history, state of the universe, and the play of subatomic particles.*

The subplot fails to mention that such neural responses are informed by and dependent upon information framed and formulated by meaning, concepts, significance, and interpretation – non-physical factors which aren't found in the laws of physics but which manage to structure, organize, and characterize the conditions and circumstances to which such neural activity must respond, and without which it wouldn't know what to respond to.

- **Subplot Four:** *Thoughts, beliefs, meaning, purpose, reason, and values are passive causal byproducts of physical events incapable of influencing how physical reality unfolds.*

The subplot fails to mention that determinists actively employ their own thoughts and beliefs to influence those of their audience, calling upon meaning, purpose, reason, values, and other non-physical concepts in the effort to convince others in the merits of determinist doctrine – an audience whose beliefs they nevertheless maintain were predetermined and must be whatever they were predestined to be.

- **Subplot Five:** *Determinism attributes our thoughts and beliefs to unthinking physical causes beyond our control, including everything we take to be true.*

  The subplot fails to note that determinist claims are no less causally compelled than any other belief one might be caused to think true. By their own terms, determinists concede they are caused to believe in determinism and believe it because they must, not because it's true. The subplot neglects to mention that determinism reduces all beliefs to causal forces beyond our control, including what we believe true and why we believe so – thus removing any rational basis for believing anything true and invalidating all truth claims, including those made by determinists.

State of Science

Each subplot contains its own lapses of logic and departures from plausibility, including failure to take into account the *current state of science*:

- *Science doesn't yet know whether the universe is deterministic or probabilistic.*

- *Causation is barred from fundamental cosmic events by relativity and quantum science.*

- *Time runs in both directions under the laws of physics, without a forward "arrow of time" required for causes to precede effects.*

- *Whether micro-level determinism requires predetermined behavior at macro-level reality is scientifically unknown.*

- *The existence of "causal necessity" can't be derived from observing regularly recurring appearances amongst contiguous events.*

- *The extent to which the appearance of causation may depend on the structure of the human mind is unknown.*

- *Nothing was predetermined at the Big Bang if quantum indeterminacy reflects how reality unfolds; and if it doesn't, predetermination is nevertheless precluded by the absence of fixed spacetime coordinates needed for successive global states of the universe.*

- *Science hasn't validated determinism and hasn't ruled out free will. Many acclaimed physicists refuse to contend otherwise.*

Nature of Matter

Further gaps in the causal narrative concern assumptions about the *nature of matter* which lack scientific validation and remain speculative:

- *The nature of matter is unknown. Whether it consists of waves, particles, both, neither, strings, quantum fields, or something yet to be discovered is an open question.*

- *Understanding the mechanics of causation is barred for lack of knowledge about what constitutes matter - i.e., that upon and through which causation would operate.*

- *The assignment of elementary particles is tentative, the Standard Model cataloguing such elements containing more than a dozen unexplained variations for which there is no scientific resolution.*

- *95% of matter in the universe hasn't been seen or verified, but which by all indicators behaves unlike any other known element or force understood by physics.*

- *Energy exists in empty space and matter arising from fields resting at zero-point energy - suggesting that matter may be some sort of potential, i.e., something other than physical substance.*

Nature of Consciousness

Finally, narrative plausibility in the causal odyssey is marred by presumptions concerning the *nature of consciousness* and how it relates to physical reality:

- *Consciousness is considered the ultimate cosmic mystery. Its nature and mechanics implicate a host of complex, unresolved questions, both scientific and philosophical.*

- *How conscious experience arises amidst a world of physical events remains unknown.*

- *Why certain qualities of experience correlate with specific patterns of nerve excitations is a mystery.*

- *The biological role of consciousness is uncertain and its adaptive value, if any, is subject to speculation.*

- *How nexus between subjective experience and physical events and transmission of influence, in one or both directions as the case may be, is an open scientific question.*

- *The role of the observer, if any, in affecting how micro-level reality manifests and behaves is subject to interpretation and controversy.*

Can a plausible case for determinism be made?

Can free will be discredited by an informed and well-constructed causal narrative?

The case would have to begin by responding to the problems listed above. Popular determinist advocacy has yet to address them. In the decade following *Free Will's* publication, Harris has yet to address them. Sapolsky is less delinquent, but nevertheless ignores the bulk of foundational problems raised in this discussion.

Sapolsky and Harris seek to make their case by barring opposing witnesses from giving testimony. But the witnesses are still lingering in the courtroom halls, anxiously awaiting the call to take the stand and have their say.

More than a few smoking guns are likely to surface once they're allowed to testify.

All told, where does this leave us?

With only one plausible candidate and several unfit for office. Most of them are giving speeches which disqualify themselves from promising anything truthful – by their own admission, they were ghost-written by unthinking quarks.

Free will nevertheless has its own share of problems. There's no scientific proof it exists. It doesn't fit squarely into the known laws of physics. There's no known mechanism by which mental events could exert influence over physical reality. And libertarian free will faces charges of incoherence.

These are no small complaints. They must be given their due. But similar objections apply to numerous other cosmic phenomena whose existence is provisionally accepted notwithstanding minimal or no understanding. Given that it's our most frequent and immediate experience, one would think holding free will to a higher standard would require justification. While quick to rely on speculation about open scientific matters, popular determinist advocacy doesn't seem much concerned about double-standards.

On the plus side, free will has a number of appealing advantages over the other candidates:

Claiming choice exists isn't a logical contradiction. It's subject to scientific verification. It's consistent with our sense of self and how we deal with others. It so happens we live every moment of our lives *with the conviction* that we have the capacity to choose and that our choices influence the course of destiny. Studies suggest the belief in free will may have positive social influence.

Perhaps most important, free will provides the *only coherent foundation* for personal responsibility, morality, and social justice – matters of no small concern for human relations, not to mention survival of the planet.

But attractiveness isn't the measure of what's true. It could be the case that we *are* mindless biochemical machines, even if we could never know it.

Or it could be that science will ultimately validate the existence of choice, in which case the noblest of human aspirations could be achieved.

The question remains open, for the time being.

At least in *this* universe....

ENDNOTES

Preface

[1] Page references in parentheses following quotes throughout the book refer to Harris, *Free Will*, Free Press (2012).

[2] Two prior books worthy of reading were published shortly after *Free Will's* publication, *Free Will: Sam Harris Has It (Wrong)* by Barry Linetsky, and *A Response to Sam Harris* by Kurt Keefner. Sapolsky's book is too new to draw any conclusions, other than past is prologue.

Chapter Two

[1] Randomness is presumed to exist by most determinists. Hence, unless context suggests otherwise, for purposes of this discussion references to the universe being determined or causal assume that some degree of randomness is involved.

[1] *Lex Fridman* podcast #185, 2021.

[2] Ellis, George, *Top-Down Causation and Emergence*, Interface Focus, 2012. Subsequent quotes below from same.

[3] *Ibid.*, Ellis, prior footnote.

[4] *Ibid.*, Ellis, footnote 3.

[5] Ismael, Jenann, *Totality, Self-Reference, and Physics,* Oxford Philosophy of Physics, 2021, available on YouTube.

Chapter Three

[1] Sapolsky, *As If You Had A Choice,* Stanford Magazine.

[2] Summaries generally based on Broadbent, Alex, "Causation", *Internet Encyclopedia of Philosophy.*

[3] Plato used many definitions, as did Aristotle, of which one was chosen for the example.

[4] Ismael, Jenann, *Interventions Without Illusions*, Yale University video presentation, 2024, YouTube.

[5] See Dow, Phil, *Physical Causation*, Cambridge University Press, 2000, for a useful summary. Also the article referenced in footnote 3 above for a basic introduction.

[6] All Hume quotations from Hume, David, *Treatise of Human Nature,* first published 1739.

[7] Some consider Hume's objections epistemological, that we can't identify necessary connections because we can only experience regularity of appearance – which isn't saying that causation doesn't exist.

[8] Ismael, J.T., *How Physics Makes Us Free,* Oxford University Press, 2016, p. 116. Jenann has explored the problematic nature of causation in numerous writings and lectures, all of which are impressive and in many respects without parallel in popularly oriented academic discourse.

[9] The unexplained subatomic phenomenon of CP variation appears to exhibit a form of time asymmetry but isn't construed as qualifying the fundamental time-symmetric nature of the laws of physics.

[10] Ismael, J.T., *How Physics Makes Us Free*, Oxford University Press, 2016.

[11] Russell, *On the Notion of Cause,* Oxford University Press (1912). All quotes from Russell from this article.

[12] Norton, J.D., *Physics and the Constitution of Reality*, Oxford University Press, 2007.

[13] Carroll, Sean, The Big Picture, *From the Big Bang to the Meaning of Life,* Ri Channel, YouTube, 2018.

[14] See summary of "On the Notion of Cause" and New-Russellian arguments in *Causation in Physics*, Stanford Encyclopedia of Philosophy.

[15] Frank, Adam, Aeon, *Minding Matter*, 2017.

[16] Davies, Paul, *The Matter Myth*, Simon and Schuster, 1992.

[17] Carroll, Sean, *Why Almost No One Understands Quantum Mechanics and the Problems in Physics*, Hidden Forces podcast, YouTube, 2020.

[18] Krauss, Laurence, *The Edge of Knowledge,* Post Hill Press, 2023.

[19] Virtual particles aren't necessarily real in any traditional sense. See excellent discussion in the Appendix to Sean Carroll's *Something Deeply Hidden*, where they are described as mathematical conversions to help facilitate the calculation of quantum fields. According to Paul Davies, virtual particles "aren't real" but seem to have an effect. *Ibid*, footnote 10.

Chapter Four

[1] Hodgson, David, *The Mind Matters*, Clarindon Press, 1991, p. 374.

[2] Even Sean Carroll, ardent advocate of the *many worlds* theory, concedes to serious problems in accounting for what appears to be probabilistic behavior. See *YouTube* debate with David Alpert on *Robinson Podcast* #106).

[3] Henceforth *randomness* is used in the sense of true randomness, not due to ignorance of underlying causes. The balance of the chapter follows the traditional quantum view that it exists for purposes of the discussion, i.e. that the prospect opens the door for the possibility of free will, which was otherwise barred under Newtonian causal law.

[4] Assuming chaos is indeterminate, a separate issue.

[5] An inordinate amount of time is also given to proving that a lack of predictability doesn't demonstrate is indeterminate. Of course it doesn't. It may be some evidence that it's the case, but not particularly strong evidence. It's a starting point, at best, for possible indeterminacy,

to be proven by other means. One more "straw man" argument dispensed with at the cost of needless pages.

[6] The contrary position, of which there are many respected adherents, is that the problem lies with relativity – that while it may predict their existence, it breaks down when it comes to addressing such extreme conditions.

[7] According to physicist Tim Maudlin, Einstein was more upset with non-locality than the probabilistic nature of quantum reality.

[8] The wave pattern consists of bands of alternating density. This is created when a wave passes through slits and emerges as two waves which overlap and interfere with each other. The same thing happens when water passes by pylons under a peer. The density bands reflect where high points from the waves overlap and fortify each other. The spaces in between reflect where peaks and valleys from the two waves overlap and cancel each other out.

[9] Feynman, Richard.

[10] Unless stated otherwise, references to traditional or mainstream quantum interpretations refer to the Copenhagen school and the current spinoffs that subscribe to the bulk of its basics, however vague and contradictory they may be.

[11] The analogy sought to illustrate in macro-terms the preposterous consequences of the *superposition* state. But many physicists take *superposition* seriously and endorse the example as a metaphor for how reality really does work.

[12] This includes Sean Carroll, highly respected physicist, author, lecturer, Caltech professor and theorist, amongst others. See *The Big Picture*, Dutton *(2016)*. On the other hand, for obvious reasons, the theory has been called "the most implausible of all ideas ever conceived of by man". Dr. Bernard Kastrup, "Consciousness Physics", *Essentia Foundation*, *YouTube*, 2023.

[13] The example is naturally simplified. The exact correlation depends on the angle of spin that's measured. The results from certain established angles always match, from others never do, and from yet others have a statistical correspondence that varies with the angle.

[14] *Quantum tunneling* is another cosmic mystery. Particles *tunnel* right through solid barriers impossible to penetrate under Newtonian science. The molecular density should preclude passage, but particles pass on through as easily as Superman through steel. There's no known physical way they can get to the other side. But somehow, they do. Physicists don't understand how such passage is possible. Does the density of the barrier simply vanish for an instant to permit passage? Does the particle navigate in and around the subatomic structure, like a rat through a maze? Does the particle wink out of existence on one side only to wink back in on the other, like a mini–Star Trek transporter. Whatever it is, it violates the principles of Newtonian causation. And it occurs constantly and countlessly throughout the universe all the time. Indeed, we must be thankful it does: it powers the Sun and helps provide daylight and warmth.

[15] Hodgson, David, *Rationality + Consciousness* = Free Will, Oxford University Press, 2012, p. 119.

[16] "[It's] the most important and astonishing result in the history of physics". Tim Maudlin, *Lectures on Bell's Theorem*. "It's not unfair to say that quantum mechanical non-locality is one of the biggest surprises to have emerged from the whole modern scientific project since it began." David Alpert, "Quantum Theory Without Observers III", *Columbia University*, *YouTube* interview, 2012.

[17] For lack of a better term, "influence" referring to connections not based on Newtonian causal law.

[18] Newton believed such non-causal influence existed, e.g. gravity – but that they were inexplicable "occult influences" beyond the pale of scientific understanding.

[19] Hobson, *Ibid.*, p. 117.

[20] A main objective concerns whether the experiments have the required *statistical independence* to correlate such distant results to support the spooky action conclusion. See Sabine Hossenfelder's presentation, "Superdeterminism", in her podcast, *Science Without the Gobbledygook.*

[21] For one of the best discussions on the lack of resolution and why experimental validation isn't possible due to the state of technology, see *Robinson* podcast, "David Alpert and Tim Maudlin: The Philosophical Foundations of Quantum Theory" (2023).

[22] Carroll, Sean, *Quantum Physics, the Multiverse, and Time Travel,* Robinson Erhardt podcast, July 2023.

[23] Greene, Brian, *World Science Festival* and The Fabric of the Universe, Knopf, 2004, p. 456.

Chapter Five

[1] Unless context suggests otherwise, for purposes of this chapter decision, conscious decision, choice, etc. is used agnostically, referring to the experience of deciding without regard to whether it's an actual free will'd decision.

[2] Ibid., Sapolsky, pages 29-30.

[3] Harris does mention the timing problem, but his point was about how our feelings of agency can be inaccurate, not the fact that this methodological problem serves to undermine the validity of all the findings he cites.

[4] The one that does, Libet, changed his mind based on subsequent testing, as discussed subsequently. Libet, "Unconscious Cerebral Initiative and the Role of Conscious Will in Voluntary Action", *Behavioral and Brain Sciences* (1985), pp. 529-66.

[5] One problematic study quoted by *Free Will* reported correlations of 80%. No subsequent study has taken place under like conditions, and

its methodological and other flaws, are discussed specifically later in this Chapter.

[6] Studies are referred to by the first author named.

[7] Unless the context is otherwise, "decisions" or "conscious decisions" references the experience of deciding, regardless of whether illusory or real.

[8] Libet, "Unconscious Initiative and the Role of Conscious Will in Voluntary Action", *Behavioral and Brain Sciences* (1985), pp. 529-66.

[9] Ibid., footnote 5.

[10] Libet, B., "Do We Have Free Will?", *Journal of Consciousness Studies,* [online], (1999), 6(8-9),, pp. 47-57.

[11] There is at least one other such study, but the focus was upon subjective accuracy, not about neural pattern impulses specific to the veto. Kuhn, Brass, "Retrospective Construction of the Judgement of Free Choice", *Consciousness and Cognition* (2009), 18(1):12-21, presents evidence it interprets to challenge the *Libet* veto. Different contexts of decisions were constructed: *impulsive* decisions (immediate responses to go signal), and *veto decisions* (immediate response to stop signal), and deliberate (decide signal to stop or not). The timing of the second signal varied, sometimes not permitting enough time for the subject to follow the cue. The signal patterns were different, however, when the subjects reported having enough time to make a conscious decisions versus making an impulsive one. The conclusion was that subjects are often confused about whether the veto was deliberate or impulsive, which seems to make any veto reporting suspect. Harris' selective presentation of the neuroscience fails to take stock of data which supports his position. Either way, his one sentence analysis of Libet's veto is inaccurate and his one sentence declaration that the Libet veto is "absurd on its face" doesn't consider the actual data, which present conflicting evidence about a post-RP veto. (Footnote 2)

[12] Ibid., footnote 5.

[13] All quotes from Mind Time, The Temporal Factor in Consciousness, Harvard University Press, 2005.

[14] J.D. Haynes, "Decoding and Predicting Intentions", *Ann. NY Acad. Sci.* (2011),1224(1):9-21.

[15] The study "headlines" referred to are Free will's close paraphrasing of the original study description.

[16] Ibid., Haynes, p. 58 (underscoring added).

[17] As quoted in Smith, *Nature*, see footnote 21, Chapter 2, Determined.

[18] Fried, Mukamel, Kreiman, "Internally Correlated Preactivation of Single Neurons in Human Medial Front Cortex Predicts Volition", *Neuron* (2011), *Neuron*, 69:548-562.

[19] Only four had electrodes in the SMA-p area, and only six in the pre-SMA (two overlapped). *Fried*, Supplemental Materials, Table One.

[20] Ibid, Fried.

[21] Fried, Supplemental Materials, Figure S-5 – 7. S

[22] The manner and methodology behind *Fried* "most" statement also wasn't disclosed.

[23] Ibid., Fried, p. 170.

[24] Ibid, Smith quoting Roskies.

[25] Ibid., Fried.

[26] Many other fanciful examples can be found on the internet by searching "correlation".

[27] Ibid., Haynes, p. 168.

[28] The Moore study found that subjects underestimated time frames for both voluntary and involuntary movements. Moore, Lagnado, "Feelings of Control: Contingency Determines Experience of Action", *Cognition* (2009) Vol 110: 2, p. 279-283. The Banks study found that timing estimates changed if the tone associated with the button press was delayed. Banks, Isham, "We Infer Rather than Perceive the Moment We Decide to Act" (2009),, *Psychological Science*, p. 657-670. The Klein study

reviewed *Libet's* data and concluded that subjects had a significant degree of uncertainty about timing matters. Klein, *Consciousness Studies/Neuroscience* (2002) 1, Wikibooks. The Danquah study concluded that timing accuracy varied based on the stimulus triggering the time measurement and the speed of the clock. Danquah, "Biases in the Subjective timing of Perceptual Events", *Consciousness and Cognition* (2008), 17:3, 616-627. Lau concluded the subjects inaccurately estimated movement time, moving it at least 50ms earlier than when it happened, in part fooled by paying more attention to the start of the movement. Lau, Rogers, Passingham, Journal *of Neuroscience* (2006), 26 (27)7265-7271. Rigoni found that the RP could be changed by focusing subjects on free will beliefs before the test. Those oriented to beliefs that free will does not exist had a reduced magnitude in RP. Rigoni, Brass, "From Intentions to Neurons", *Topoi* (2013), 33, 5-12.

[29] Ibid., *Fried*.

[30] Annual Meeting of the Neurophilosophy of Free Will Consortium, seminars 2020 and 2022, available on *YouTube*.

[31] See quotes from studies discussed in the next section regarding contrary science findings.

[32] Hermann, Pauen, "Analysis of a Choice Reaction Task Yields a New Interpretation of Libet's Experiments", *Korea University* (2008), 151-157.

[33] Trevena, Miller, "Cortical Movement Preparation Before and After a Conscious Decision to Move", *Consciousness and Cognition* (2002), 11(2) 162-90, 314-325.

[34] Ibid., Sapolsky, pages 27.

[35] "Libet studies" and similar terms are often used to refer to the line of similar studies that followed in *Libet's* wake.

[36] Hodgson, David, *Rationality + Consciousness* = Free Will, Oxford University Press, 2012, p. 148.

[37] Bizzi, Emilio and Ajemian, Robert, "A Hard Scientific Quest: Understanding Voluntary Movements", *Daedalus, Journal of American Arts and Sciences, Winter Edition* (2015).

[38] Schurger, Sitt, Deheane, "An Accumulator Model for Spontaneous Neural Activity", *Cognitive Imaging Unit*, INSERM, *PNAS* (2012), *Early Edition*.

[39] Haggard, Libet, "Conscious Intention and Brain Activity", *Journal of Consciousness Studies* (2001), 8(11), 47-64.

[40] Herman, Pauen, "Analysis of a Choice Reaction Task", *Intl. Journal of Psychophysiology* (2007), 67:2, 151-7.

[41] Ibid., Trevena.

[42] Schultze, Kraft, Rusconi, Haynes, "Point of No Return in Vetoing Self-Initiated Movements", *Biological Sciences* (2015), 113:4.

[43] They can all be readily found online, along with many summaries and commentaries.

[44] An exception or two includes replication of the original Libet test, along with replications which have discounted RP in favor of LRP, same neural signal from the opposite lob of movement.

[45] One study tracked choices to spend for charity versus other purposes whose findings were contrary to determinist claims of neural brain causation.

Chapter Six

[1] Penrose, Roger, *The Emperor's New Mind*, Random House, 1994.

[2] David Alpert, Where Philosophy Meets Science, *Big Think*, YouTube, 2012.

[3] Carroll, Sean, Mindscape podcast, Episode 9, Why is There Something Rather Than Nothing?, YouTube, 2019.

[4] Smolin, Lee, Quantum Gravity, Persius Books, 2001.

[5] Leonard Susskind, "Is the Universe Fine Tuned for Life and Mind?", *YouTube* video (2013).

[6] Feynman, Richard, widely quoted without source, *Wikipedia* cites "The Character of Physical Law", transcript of *Cornell University* lecture (2014).

[7] *Ibid.*, footnote 18, Chapter Five.

[8] Kraus, Lawrence, Robinson Podcast, "God, String Theory, and the State of Physics", YouTube, 2024

[9] Chomsky, Noam, Free Will, "Chomsky's Philosophy", *YouTube,* posted 2015.

[10] *Ibid.*

[11] Ismael, Jennan, *Physics and Free Will*, The Free Will Show, Episode 29, YouTube.

[12] Einstein was a determinist, but as noted by Tim Maudlin, he wasn't troubled by the indeterminacy of quantum mechanics and may have ultimately come to accept it had he lived long enough. (Numerous *YouTube* podcast interviews concerning the foundations of quantum mechanics.)

[13] Hodgson, David, *Ibid.*, p. 142.

[14] Susskind, Leonard, *The Black Hole Wars*, Blackstone Audio, 2008, Chapter 6.

[15] Robinson Podcast 198, *The Mantaculus,(Or a Probability Map of the Universe*, 2024,YouTube.

[16] Emergence comes in two flavors. *Weak* emergence reduces higher level structures to their component parts and supports determinist doctrine. *Strong* emergence permits the possibility of free will and is the subject of this section. Hence references to "emergence", "emergent theory", etc. refers to *strong emergence*.

[17] *Ibid.*, Ellis, footnote 3, Chapter Two.

[18] *Ibid.*, Ismael, footnote 9.

[19] His "second" and "third" objections are one and the same.

[20] *Ibid.*, Ismael.

[21] Sabine Hassenfelder, "You Don't Have *Free Will*, But Don't Worry", *Physics Without the Gobbledygook, YouTube* video.

[22] *Ibid.*, Ismael.

[23] Most references to "science" is to the hard sciences, unless the context suggests a broader scope.

[24] Schrodinger, E., 1952, cited in *The Many Worlds of Hugh Everett III*.

[25] Section inspired by the works of Thomas Nagel, including Views from Nowhere.

[26] *Ibid.*, prior footnote.

Chapter Seven

[1] Such claims have various names, including self-defeating, self-refuting, performative contradictions, etc. Some are used for logical contradictions, others for those whose premises undermine what the claim is saying.

[2] The self-defeating issue is nevertheless alive and well in historical and academic circles, e.g. see Castagnoli, Luca, *Ancient Self-Refutation*, Cambridge University Press, 2010; works of Jurgen Habermas, who liberally uses self-refutation to discredit post-modernism and other philosophical movements. Ken Wilber mentions it in an interview by *The Integral Institute* posted on YouTube. Thomas Nagel bases many of his critiques on self-refutational arguments.

[3] Percy Prior podcast, YouTube, October 2013.

[4] *Ibid.*, Thomas Nagel quoting Hillary Putnam.

[5] Chomsky, Noam, "Lectures on Matter and Mind, and Mind: The Machine, the Ghost, and the Limits of Understanding", *MIT Lectures*, YouTube posts (2019).

Chapter Nine

[1] Unless responsibility is taken to mean actions which emanate from the person, which is one accepted usage for the word but true of reflexes and any other unconscious action or reaction – which isn't the kind of responsibility relevant to the free will debate.

[2] Three of these constitute the famous legal McNaughton test for sanity.

[3] Harris, *The Moral Landscape* (2010).

Chapter Eight

[1] Hodgson, David, *Rationality + Conscousness = Free Will*, Oxford University Press, 2012, p. 109.

[2] "Utilitarian" is used in this discussion to refer to practical decisions that have utility in the achievement of ends, *not to* the moral theory about maximizing "utility", in the sense of the greatest good for the greatest number, or increasing well-being.

[3] *Ibid.*, Introduction, p. xi.

Chapter Ten

[1] Observation and introspection are used synonymously, the first directed to external reality and the latter internal.

[2] Hodgson, David, *Ibid.*

[3] Agency in the Stream of Consciousness, *Talks in Neuroscience on Free Will*, 2020, available on YouTube.

[4] Barrett, "The Future of Psychology: Connecting Mind to Brain", *Perspectives on Psychological Science* (2009), 326-339.

[5] Thompson, Evan, "Looping Effects and the Cognitive Science, Meditation", *Buddhism and Science* (2017), 47.

[6] Hutchins, "Mindfulness Meditation", *Journal of Evidence Based Alternative Medicines* (2011, 2019),13:1, p.34-35.

[7] Eller, Jonathan, *Becoming Ray Bradbury*, University of Illinois Press (1952).

Chapter Thirteen

[1] Vohs, Schooler, "The Value of Believing in Free Will", *Psychological Science* (2008), 19:1, p. 49-54.

[2] Baumeister, Masicampo, DeWall, "Prosocial Benefits of Free Will", *Personality and Social Psychology Bulletin*, 35: 260-268.

[3] Shariff, Greene, Karremans, "Free Will and Punishment" APS (2014),, 25:8, 1563-70.

[4] Krueger, Hoffman, Walter, Grafman, "An fMRI Investigation of the Effects of the Belief in Free Will on Third-Party Punishment", *Oxford Academic* (2013),9:8, 1149-53.

[5] Casper, Vuillaume, Gama, Cleermans, "The Influence of Disbelief in Free Will on Immoral Behavior", *Frontier Psychology*, (2017)17:8, eCollection.

Chapter Fourteen

[1] The probabilistic aspects of quantum mechanics have put a dent in the scientific acceptance of determinist doctrine.

Made in the USA
Las Vegas, NV
03 June 2024